Block IX   George Grosz and Weimar Germany

Contents

Set reading

Herschel B. Chipp, *Theories of Modern Art*, University of California Press, 1975.

George Heard Hamilton, *Painting and Sculpture in Europe 1880–1940*, Penguin Books, 1981.

Francis Frascina and Charles Harrison (eds), *Modern Art and Modernism: A Critical Anthology*, Harper and Row, 1982 (referred to as the Reader).

You should read the following extracts from the Reader in the course of working through Block IX:

32 W. Benjamin, 'The Author as Producer'

33 W. Benjamin, 'The Work of Art in the Age of Mechanical Reproduction'

35 B. Brecht, 'Popularity and Realism'.

You will also need to read the relevant extracts in the *Supplementary Documents*.

Broadcasting

The following programmes are broadcast while you are working on Block IX.

Television programme 19   *Klee and the Revolution*
Television programme 20   *Authority, Regression and Representation in Painting*
Radiovision programme 19   *Berlin and Dada*
Radiovision programme 20   *Heartfield*

You should look at the notes and illustrations which accompany these programmes before the broadcasts.

The following broadcasts are also relevant to this Block.

Television programme 10   *Kirchner and Berlin*
Television programme 18   *The 1922 Russian Exhibition in Berlin*
Television programme 21   *Beckmann*
Radiovision programme 15   *A Marxist Aesthetic*
Radiovision programme 16   *Marxism and Art*

THE OPEN UNIVERSITY
Arts: A Third Level Course
Modern Art and Modernism:
Manet to Pollock

BLOCK IX (Units 19–20)

George Grosz and Weimar Germany

Prepared for the Course Team by Gill Perry

The Open University Press

The Open University Press
Walton Hall
Milton Keynes
MK7 6AA

First published 1983. Reprinted 1988.

Designed by the Graphic Design Group of the Open University.

Text set in 12/13½pt Garamond Medium

Printed in Great Britain by Louis Drapkin Ltd., Birmingham B9 4EA.

ISBN 0 335 111130.

This text forms part of an Open University course. The complete list of the course appears at the end of this text.

For general availability of supporting material referred to in this text, please write to Open University Educational Enterprises Limited, 12 Cofferidge Close, Stony Stratford, Milton Keynes, MK11 1BY, Great Britain.

Further information on Open University courses may be obtained from the Admissions Office, The Open University, PO Box 48, Walton Hall, Milton Keynes, MK7 6AB.

1.2

List of illustrations associated with Block IX

(These are provided in separate booklets. You should refer to the captions printed with the plates for full details of the pictures.)

Colour plates

Black-and-white plates

Introduction

In the preceding block on Russian Art and the Revolution you were introduced to a new set of issues in the history of modern art: the debates associated with attempts to redefine an art practice within a post-revolutionary socialist society. In this block we will look at related issues that preoccupied some groups of artists working in Weimar Germany, especially the problem of how to define and carry out a 'socialist' art practice within a capitalist society.

This problem is continually raised in some of the writings of George Grosz, who was working in Berlin after the First World War, during the period of Weimar government. In this block, we will consider the relationship of Grosz's art practice, particularly his graphic work, to his own and other contemporary theoretical ideas about politically committed art or (as Grosz called it) *'Tendenzkunst'* (literally translated as 'tendentious art'). We will also look (albeit selectively) at the ways in which Grosz's works were received and assessed by the German public and critics both during the Weimar period and in subsequent art history, considering some interpretations of his work as, for example, 'realist', 'socialist', 'degenerate' and in some cases 'Modernist'.

A major assumption behind the content and structure of this block is that the issues and practices which preoccupied Grosz are firmly rooted in the specific political and social situation of the Weimar period. Although very different to the sequence of events in Russia, there were many developments in Germany in the immediate post-war years that could be seen to constitute a revolutionary situation. With the defeat of Germany in 1918, Kaiser Wilhelm II abdicated. In that year the position of Reichs Chancellor was taken up by Friedrich Ebert, President of the Social Democratic Party (SPD), and the Weimar Republic (named after the city of Weimar which became the political capital) was officially established. There followed a period of intense political strife and polarization when the German Communist Party (KPD), of which Grosz was a founder member in 1918, looked to the Russian Revolution as a model to follow, and concentrated its efforts against the ruling SPD. It should be noted that membership of the German Communist Party at this time meant something rather different to being a member of the British Communist Party today. The KPD was viewed with suspicion by the ruling SPD and even outlawed for a period in 1923. And during the so-called 'November Revolution', which we discuss later in this block, many of its leaders were murdered. Propaganda produced both by the right wing and the social democrats played on the associations with Russia and the notion of a 'bolshevist' conspiracy infiltrating Germany through the KPD (Figures 1 and 2). As we shall see, 'bolshevism' became an emotive and derogatory label which was used by conservatives to symbolize various forms of social anarchism and depravity.

In this block, we will try to show how a knowledge of the nature of the German 'left', of the expectations of many Germans in the years after the armistice of 1918, and of the social and political issues which dominated public debates, is important for an understanding of Grosz's work and interests at the time. In much of his painted and graphic work, particularly his satirical drawings, from this period, Grosz addresses some of these issues. A problem for this block (and for many others in the course) is in how we relate the social history to the actual drawings and paintings. In some works, such as those drawings that satirize political figures (**Pl.IX.1** and Figure 16) there are clear causal links between the subject matter and contemporary political or social events. But in those paintings and drawings in which the imagery is more complex or less specific in terms of what is represented (**Pls.IX. 2 and 3**), we have to be more cautious when relating works to specific

Volksgenossen!

Arbeiter!   Soldaten!

Wölfe im Schafspelz sind die **Spartakus-Bolschewisten,** die Euch ein Schlaraffenland versprechen und Euch zu frechen Gewalttaten mißbrauchen!

In dem bösen Wirrwarr dieser Tage rettet doch wenigstens **Euren eigenen Verstand!**

Die Spartakisten sind nicht idealgesinnte Sozialisten, wie sie naiven Leuten einzureden versuchen, sondern ganz gewöhnliche Abenteurer, deren offen erklärte Absicht es ist,

mit den Russen gemeinsam am deutschen Rhein gegen Franzosen und Engländer zu kämpfen! Also nicht Frieden und Brot, sondern neuen blutigen Krieg und verschärfte Hungersnot!

Wer bisher gleichgültig dem wüsten Treiben der Liebknecht-Luxemburg-Sippschaft zusah, muß nunmehr endlich erkennen, was uns bevorsteht, wenn die Bolschewisten und ihre verlogenen Hintermänner die Oberhand bekommen:

Arbeiter, Soldaten, die ihr den grausigen Krieg aus eigener Erfahrung kennen gelernt habt!

Westdeutschland wird Kriegsgebiet!

Das bedeutet Verwüstungen und Verheerungen wie in Flandern und Nordfrankreich. Städte und Dörfer werden in Trümmer sinken, namenloses Unglück ihren Bewohnern bereitend!

Das ganze Reich wird Aufmarschgelände und Etappengebiet für die russischen Heere!

Denkt an die russischen Greueltaten in Ostpreußen 1914. **Berlin wird Hauptquartier** der russischen „roten Armee", **der Trotzki, Lenin** und der anderen Räuberhauptmänner des asiatischen Terrors! — Die selber Hunger leidenden Russen sollen uns mit Lebensmittel versorgen! Wer glaubt das?

Deutschland soll ein zweites Rußland werden,

d. h. völliger politischer und wirtschaftlicher Zusammenbruch, allgemeine Arbeitslosigkeit, größte Not und schlimmstes Massenelend!

Massenmord und Seuchen würden unser Land bald in einen großen Friedhof verwandeln! Damit wäre das „Ideal" der anti-sozialen Terroristen verwirklicht!

Arbeiter! Soldaten! Erkennt die Gefahr solange es noch Zeit ist!

Genossenschaftsbruckerei und sozialpolitischer Verlag Berlin SW

Figure 1 SPD poster attacking the Spartacus movement. The headlines read:

COMRADES!
WORKERS!   SOLDIERS!
THE SPARTACUS-BOLSHEVISTS ARE WOLVES IN SHEEP'S CLOTHING!
GERMANY WILL BECOME A WAR ZONE!
THEY WANT GERMANY TO BECOME A SECOND RUSSIA!

From Weimarer Republik, *ed. vom Kunstamt Kreuzberg, Berlin, and the Institut für Theaterwissenschaft der Universität Köln, 2nd edn., Elefanten Press Verlag, Berlin, 1977, p.134.*

Es hat keinen Wert, um Dinge die sind, herumzureden: Es ist feige — daher undeutsch — Tatsachen auszuweichen, die täglich frecher sich zeigen:

Der Bolschewismus ist der neueste Trumpf der Juden. Spartakus

ist nichts weiter als der

Judaskuss,

den die als Schnorrer zu uns gekommenen Hebräer dem christlichen deutschen Volke um fremdes Geld aufdrückten! Ihrem Moderatent fügten die Juden aller Branchen die holde Zunft der Marodeure Zuhälter, und des Berliner Pöbels hinzu, um ihre brutale, staat- und kirchenfeindliche jüdische Gewaltherrschaft auf den Trümmern friedlicher deutscher Heimstätten aufzubauen!

Wie lange soll das Treiben noch angehen?

Hat das verratene, aus unzähligen Wunden blutende und von außen und innen mehr denn je bedrohte Deutschland noch nicht genug gelitten?

Wollen wir, die wir alles, alles opferten, uns noch in den Bürgerkrieg hetzen lassen, uns zerfleischen, während das Volk Israel unsere heiligsten Werte schamlos mit Füßen tritt?

Bolschewismus ist die neueste Fabrikmarke für Judaismus!

Das merkt Euch, Deutsche Männer und Frauen, in Stadt und Land. — Es hat keinen Wert, um Dinge die sind, herumzureden!

Wache auf, deutsche Christenheit! Schütze Deine Heiligtümer!

Figure 2 Anti-Spartacus poster, probably printed by a right-wing anti-Jewish group. The headlines read:

BOLSHEVISM IS THE LATEST TRUMP-CARD OF THE JEWS.
SPARTACUS is nothing more than the JUDAS KISS
BOLSHEVISM IS THE LATEST TRADEMARK FOR JUDAISM!
WAKE UP, GERMAN CHRISTENDOM! PROTECT ALL THAT IS SACRED TO YOU!

From Weimarer Republik, op.cit., *p.134.*

developments in social history, seeking to avoid crude or over-simplified causal links.

Clearly, the aims outlined above demand familiarity with, and discussion of, the complicated social and historical developments in Germany during the Weimar period. To help give an outline of the events of this period, a brief chronological chart has been reproduced as Appendix A. Both this and the historical material discussed in the block are far from exhaustive. They have been selected largely for the purposes of this case study on Grosz and the related arguments and debates. For a broader picture of social and historical developments during this period you are recommended to read J. Willett, *The New Sobriety: Art and Politics in the Weimar Period 1917–33*, Thames and Hudson, London, 1978, and Peter Gay, *Weimar Culture*, Penguin, London, 1968.

Why Grosz in a course on modern art and Modernism?

In earlier blocks you have seen how a coherent body of criticism and discourse about art helped to establish a German avant-garde which we now associate with the broad label 'Expressionist', an avant-garde preoccupied with non-figurative art as the expression of spiritual or emotional forces. In this block we will be considering the view that Grosz's work forms an alternative to 'Expressionism', and is in this sense 'anti-Modernist'. But to designate something as anti-Modernist assumes that there is a coherent theory or view of Modernism to be opposed. Modernism has evolved as a theory of modern art, and although Grosz's writings seem to focus on many of those issues and oppositions with which we are concerned in this course, his view of the art world and its divisions reflects his own historical situation in Germany in the 1920s, and is different to the picture of Modernism that might be constructed by this course team writing in the 1980s.

The Weimar period of German art is characterized (broadly speaking) by a confusion and fragmentation of attitudes and artistic styles which had previously constituted the 'Expressionist' avant-garde. Grosz's work from the Weimar period, like that of many contemporary *Neue Sachlichkeit* painters (a loose category literally translated as 'New Objectivity' or 'New Realism', which is discussed later in this block) is frequently categorized as anti-Modernist on the basis of what it looks like. The figurative styles employed by George Grosz, Otto Dix or Max Beckmann (**Col.pls.IX.II and 12**) for example, are often opposed to the more abstract art of painters such as Kandinsky or Delaunay who were both being exhibited in Germany at the time.

For example, if you look at a painting by Grosz from 1917, *Burial; Dedicated to Oscar Panizza* (**Col.pl.IX.1**) and compare it with a Kandinsky painting, *Picture with a White Border*, 1912 (**Col.pl.VII.1**), it is easy to see these two paintings as representing opposing interests. In the *Dedication to Oscar Panizza*, which is discussed more fully on pp.32–3, social and historical references are signposted in the more clearly readable figurative style. Although there is some formal distortion, we can identify different types of figures including a skeleton, middle-class men in bowler hats, a priest, etc. In the Kandinsky, on the other hand, the combination of lines, shapes and colours is less easily read. It is much more difficult to identify recognizable objects in the Kandinsky, and therefore easier to locate it in terms of aesthetic issues rather than social or historical ones.

As you saw in the discussion of abstract art in Block VII, some Modernist histories of art have tended to see 'representational' or figurative art as antithetical to 'abstract' art. You should recall that Barr, who is quoted in Block VII, p.7, claims that abstract art evolved because 'the most adventurous and original artists had grown bored with painting facts. By a common and powerful impulse they were driven to abandon the imitation of natural appearances'. Not only is a qualitative distinction made here between the two types of art, but the origins of abstract art are systematically explained in terms of 'impulses', formal developments and technical innovations, with little regard for the influence of historical and material conditions.

In writing about his art, Grosz exploited the idea of an 'opposition of styles', but for rather different reasons from Barr's. He was writing as a practising artist rather than an art historian, and in his writings from the early twenties he understood the conflict in terms of opposed political commitments. He consistently rejected what he saw as an Expressionist preoccupation with spiritual values and 'individual expression', setting up a clear distinction between what he called an 'Expressionist anarchism' and a committed art:

> The anarchism of Expressionism must stop! Today painters are forced into this situation because they are unenlightened and have no links with working people.

But a time will come when artists — instead of being scrubby bohemian anarchists — will be clean, healthy workers in a collectivist community.

(G. Grosz, *My New Pictures*, 1920, *Supplementary Documents*, IX.5.)

Grosz had little sympathy for even those Expressionist artists who aligned themselves with the left immediately after the First World War:

When the tide seemed to turn, the most esoteric brushes discovered their hearts beating for the working masses, and for a few months, red and pale pink allegories and pamphlets were produced in large numbers. But soon, law and order returned, and, lo and behold, our artists noiselessly made their way back to the higher spheres.

(Grosz and Herzfelde, *Art is in Danger*, 1925, quoted in Hans Hess, *George Grosz*, 1974, p.84.)

Grosz is probably referring here to, amongst others, some of those Expressionist artists who in 1918–19 associated themselves with radical artists' groups such as the *Novembergruppe* and the *Arbeitsrat für Kunst* (Workers' Council for Art) discussed on p.27. Grosz probably joined the *Novembergruppe* when it was formed in 1918 (it is often difficult to establish when he joined various organizations as he rarely commented on them in his writings). Other founder members included the painters Max Pechstein, Rudolf Schlichter and Otto Dix. Their founding manifesto (reproduced in *Supplementary Documents*, IX.1), opened with the emotional claim:

We are standing on the fertile soil of the revolution. Our slogan is: Freedom, Equality and Fraternity!

In January 1919 the group published its 'Guidelines' (see *Supplementary Documents*, IX.2) defining itself as 'an alliance of radical artists' and outlining revolutionary plans to reorganize art schools and museums in Germany. The failure to achieve many of these aims led to the formation within the group of a left-wing opposition, with which Grosz identified himself. They wrote an open letter (*Supplementary Documents*, IX.4), published in Wieland Herzfelde's left-wing magazine *Der Gegner*, attacking the *Novembergruppe* for failing to carry out its revolutionary intentions and rejecting the tendency of many of its members to dream of spiritual utopias and 'higher spheres'. These preoccupations were incompatible with Grosz's desire in 1921 to 'be caught up by the ideas of working people and help them in the struggle against a corrupt society' (*Instead of a Biography*).

In his written and reported statements from the early 1920s, Grosz continually opposes his art to that of those artists preoccupied with spiritual goals. For him the problem revolves around a notion of 'political art' or '*Tendenzkunst*'.

The dispute within the *Novembergruppe* was centred around different notions of the function of art in contemporary German society. The left-wing faction was preoccupied with the idea of *Tendenzkunst*. In post-war Germany the term assumed a more specific meaning than merely 'tendentious art', signifying instead an art that is political, having a propagandist function. The view held by many German artists who opposed Grosz and his colleagues was that *Tendenzkunst* was a Marxist concept, and that an art which consciously involved itself with social and political issues was a *transitory* and contingent art. It should be concerned instead with supposedly more enduring problems of style and artistic expression. This view is rooted in the early Expressionist theories of art discussed in Block IV.

The debate was partly generated by differing definitions of the term 'political art'. It is frequently used loosely by art historians to denote different sorts of interests. For example, there can be a difference between the *conscious* production of art as political propaganda and the interpretation of art as political, although the dividing line between the two may be blurred. A work in which the artist did not consciously intend to make a political or propagandist point may nevertheless be interpreted as political or propagandist. The way in which a work is understood depends largely on the context in which it is consumed and the interests it encounters. As you have seen in earlier blocks, there were many critics in the late nineteenth and early twentieth centuries who equated an unconventional style with a 'revolutionary' or 'anarchistic' frame of mind. (See, for example, some reactions to the Fauves, described in Block IV.) This was to confuse technical radicalism with a social critique.

This use implies a vague notion of 'political' which is loosely equated with political anarchism. In post-war Germany, on the other hand, 'political art' was also frequently used to signify attitudes more clearly associated with specific party political views. In several of his written statements (*Supplementary Documents*, IX.3 and 5), Grosz, like many other members of the German Communist Party, understood *Tendenzkunst* to mean an art that is necessarily rooted in the class conflict between the 'masses' and the bourgeoisie.

For Grosz and other communist artists who signed the open letter of protest to the *Novembergruppe* in 1921, there was a sense in which the division between 'political' and 'non-political' art was meaningless. Following a Marxist analysis of 'culture', they argued that all art, irrespective of its content and aims, is implicitly political. As art was part of the social, political and cultural 'superstructure' of society, it must always reflect either directly or indirectly the determinations of the material and economic 'base' which supported it. According to this argument, all art is either conscious or unconscious *Tendenzkunst*. Those art forms that do not serve the interests of the proletariat are implicitly supporting the capitalist system. Grosz believed it was the responsibility of a Marxist artist to produce a proletarian art that would 'help the working class in their struggle against a rotten society' (*Instead of a Biography*, 1920, *Supplementary Documents*, IX.3).

This raised the problem of how to produce a genuine 'proletarian art' within and through the existing conventions of capitalist culture. This problem, which dominated a good deal of contemporary debate, was focused on differing notions of 'realism' in art, and will be encountered again as a concern of the Surrealists in Block XI. It could be argued that many modern artists working within western capitalist societies, who wanted to make a clear point about contemporary society, were more likely to use 'realistic' or figurative styles and types of art through which their references and comments could be more easily recognized. Social realism, satire and caricature, although all loose categories, are groupings often associated with 'political art'.

The use of satire and caricature to make a political point dominates much of Grosz's work from the 1920s. In contemporary and subsequent writings Grosz was compared with Honoré Daumier, and frequently labelled a 'German Hogarth'. These comparisons associate his use of caricature with specific historical precedents.

To consider the relevance of such associations, look at Figures 3 and 4, and note the information in the captions.

▶ Are there similarities in the techniques, styles and subjects of these two works? Are there any art historical parallels that you would be cautious about drawing? ◀

▷ In selecting works for comparison, I deliberately chose similar themes. Both are directed towards an aspect of contemporary military activity. Daumier's *Conqueror* represents the indulgent buffoon-like character of a 'victorious' officer fighting for Napoleon III, while Grosz depicts an ugly right-wing Prussian general amidst a pile of bloody corpses. Both drawings were printed; they were designed for publication and wide popular consumption rather than as 'fine art' works to be consumed by a few. As we shall see later in this block, this was one of the reasons why Grosz was attracted to the graphic medium. It was also a reason why it was more likely to be seen by the establishment as potentially subversive.

Figure 3 Honoré Daumier, The Conqueror, *1859, lithograph, one of many plates which appeared in the series,* Actualités, *in the 1850s and 1860s. Bibliothèque Nationale, Paris.*

Figure 4 George Grosz, The White General, *c. 1923, pen and ink drawing, in* Die Pleite, *November 1923. Photo from H. Hess, George Grosz, Studio Vista, London 1974. © S.P.A.D.E.M., Paris, 1982.*

Both drawings could be seen as satirical in that they use caricature to ridicule and expose their subjects. 'Caricature' is a term normally used to signify a drawing (or painting) in which particular human characteristics are exaggerated; individual features or habits are often singled out and emphasized or distorted. It is therefore an ideal means of representation through which to criticize political developments, or to make a propagandist point.

You might argue that there are differences in the satirical content of the two drawings. Daumier's form of caricature could be seen as more humorous and gentler than that of Grosz. While the French artist has emphasized the buffoon-like stupidity of his soldier, Grosz has represented a horrifyingly cruel and despicable character. That said, we cannot make useful comparisons about forms of caricature and their critical meanings without some knowledge of the different historical circumstances in which each was produced. While both use similar conventions of exaggeration and distortion, their specific historical meanings are, of course, different.

While the Daumier was, in its time, a reference to Napoleon III's reckless military adventures in the Crimean War, in China and in Austria, the Grosz is a reference to the German bloody counter-revolution, led by generals of right-wing political persuasion, immediately after the First World War. They were produced under different forms of political censorship, which may have helped to determine the choice of subject and form of caricature. Daumier, for example, had to be particularly careful to produce images which could get past the Napoleonic régime's official censor and which would therefore be likely to be published. We also need to know how these forms of illustrations, at the times at which they were produced, related to the dominant conventions of illustration and 'high art'. These relationships affected the ways in which they were understood and received by their contemporary public. ◁

In this block, we will attempt to view Grosz's work with such concerns in mind. While on the one hand Grosz was seeking around 1920 to produce a genuine 'proletarian art', he also borrowed (in many works) from those formal conventions, such as diagonal 'lines of force' (see **Col.pls.IX.1 and 3**, and Figure 22), associated with the European avant-garde. Such borrowings have provoked Modernist readings of his works in which the formal content and graphic techniques are emphasized, while the social and political content is played down.

Grosz's expressed concern, in both his graphic and painted work, to find a formal language which could convey an intended relationship between art and politics, was directly related to the contemporary debate about what artistic forms and practices constituted 'realism' in visual art. You should recall the discussion in Block V on 'realism' and the shifting meanings of the term when used in relation to Courbet's work in the mid-nineteenth century, and later Cubist interests. And in the preceding block you were introduced to a narrow Russian notion of 'Socialist Realism'. In Weimar Germany, the *Neue Sachlichkeit* movement, with which Grosz was associated, was directly involved with a notion of a 'New Realism' in art. As we shall see, however, there were a range of art practices and differing political interests associated with this label, and in Grosz's own written statements and practical work we will find contradictory approaches to the problem. Some later attempts to provide coherent theories of the political function and nature of 'realism' in art, particularly those of the dramatist Bertolt Brecht and the writer and critic Walter Benjamin in the 1930s, will be considered in Part 3.

1 Historical and artistic background

Grosz in Berlin and the Berlin art world

A large part of Grosz's working life before 1933 (when he emigrated to America) was spent in Berlin. It was in this environment that he established himself as a graphic artist, first became actively involved in left-wing politics and then formulated and published many of his ideas on the role of art in society. In order to try to sort out some of the possible historical and artistic reasons for Grosz's interests and activities at this time, we need to look briefly at what was happening in the Berlin art world (i.e. which artists were working in Berlin, which dealers were influential and what they were exhibiting) and at developments in the social and political life of the metropolis.

In 1912, after studying fine art at the Dresden Academy of Art, Grosz moved to Berlin. The move to the metropolis was partly for economic reasons; as a Prussian citizen he was not eligible for a state scholarship or grant to finance the continuation of his studies. He enrolled at the Berlin School of Arts and Crafts, where he studied until 1917.

Once the capital of Prussia, Berlin had been the political and financial capital of the German Reich since German unification in 1871. It was now a major industrial centre with a population that had nearly doubled between 1885 and 1910 (*Hofkalender* population figures are 1,315,287 for 1885 and 2,071,257 for 1910), and by the outbreak of the First World War it had become the main centre of the German arts and entertainment worlds. Grosz had spent most of his youth in the provincial town of Stolp, and was excited by this new environment that not only gave him access to large public and private collections of modern art, but also provided him with a wealth of urban themes to illustrate.

At the Dresden Academy he had studied drawing or 'copying' as it was officially called, although his interest in illustrative drawing was then combined with an ambition to be a successful painter of great historical paintings, an aim which was shared by many other students of art in German academies at the time (see Block IV on the role of German art academies at the turn of the century). He believed that his popular drawings would win him the necessary financial success to fulfil his main ambition, a point worth noting in view of the tendency in much art criticism to see him from an early age as having been motivated almost entirely by a desire to be a graphic illustrator.

His autobiography entitled *A Little Yes and a Big No*, published in 1946, although coloured by his later changed views on art after his move to America, underlines the material reasons for his early interest in what he called 'caricatures':

> Somebody once told me that one could make a great deal of money with caricatures. Before very long this mistake was to lead to vast quantities of the most fatuous 'line-style' drawing. Most of them didn't come out of my own head anyway . . . .
>
> (*A Little Yes and a Big No*, p. 50.)

This 'line-style' ('*Linienstilistik*') was used in many drawings and illustrations executed before about 1912. It was a linear drawing technique well suited for caricatures because of its precise and detailed use of line. One of his earliest drawings in this style was published in 1910 in *Ulk*, the humorous supplement of the *Berliner Tageblatt* (Figure 5).

Figure 5 George Grosz, Holidays in Thorn, *1910, his first cartoon to be published in* Ulk, *the humorous supplement of the* Berliner Tageblatt. *Akademie der Künste, George-Grosz-Archiv, Berlin.* © *S.P.A.D.E.M., Paris, 1982.*

Grosz's early interest in graphic illustration was partly conditioned by his access to illustrated magazines as a child. In 1898, when he was four, his family had moved from Berlin to Stolp, a small provincial town in remote Pomerania. His access to the outside world was largely through the medium of illustrated magazines and newspapers. And he avidly consumed the 'penny dreadfuls', penny magazines which featured absurd tales of romance and adventure with ominous titles such as *Jack and the Mysterious Girl Slayer* (Figures 6 and 7), which was in his own collection.

In his earliest illustrations he shows the influence of those drawing styles with which he was familiar, fluctuating between a precise detailed technique reminiscent of the 'penny dreadfuls', and a simpler 'line-style' (**Pls.IX.4 and 5**). At the Dresden Academy, he absorbed much from the work of *Jugendstil* illustrators (you should recall from Block IV that Dresden was then an important centre of *Jugendstil* poster design), which encouraged him to use the freer, less detailed style that characterized the *Ulk* drawing.

After the move to Berlin, he studied under Orlik at the Berlin School of Arts and Crafts. In a different artistic and social environment his conceptions of art were changing, and he began to attach a different importance to graphic work. It was no longer seen as a means to an end, and he no longer separated detailed copying exercises (which, within the context of the Dresden Academy, provided excellent training for history painting) from popular drawings (i.e. cartoon and caricature drawings). In Berlin, which had become an important centre for graphic production, he was encouraged to see himself in the role of an illustrator, an applied artist who is not a mere 'cartoonist'. But by 1912 he was successfully publishing drawings that concentrated on themes other than those which had won him success as a 'caricaturist' and which employed different techniques. Many of his drawings from about 1912, including some of those published in the periodicals *Lustige Blätter* and *Kunst und Künstler*, are illustrations rather than caricatures of life in the Berlin suburbs (**Pls.IX.6 and 7**). These are generally less stylized and less 'cartoon'-like than the *Ulk* drawings.

*Figure 6 Illustration on title page of a 'penny dreadful',
entitled* Jack the Mysterious Girl Slayer *formerly owned
by Grosz. Verlag Gerd Hatje, Stuttgart.*

*Figure 7 Title page of a 'penny dreadful', 1907. Verlag
Gerd Hatje, Stuttgart.*

He no longer measured his artistic competence in terms of his ability to produce
'high' art easel paintings. His letters and records from this time show him to be
increasingly preoccupied with his role as an illustrator, which led him to experi-
ment with new drawing techniques and methods of reproduction:

> Gradually my style changed a little. How that came about I do not know myself: I
> suppose it was for technical reasons of reproduction. Now I first carefully drew the
> contours of figure in steady line and then washed the whole drawing with graphic
> ink at random and yet in a craftsmanlike manner . . . I also began to use a thick
> pointed drawing pen . . . My ambitious boyhood plans of gigantic oil paintings,
> easels on scaffolds and brushes the size of brooms had receded into the background.
>
> (A Little Yes and a Big No, p. 87.)

How are these changes in Grosz's work and attitudes related to other developments
in his social and political outlook at the time? His letters from 1912–15 (particularly his series to Robert Bell) show a growing dissatisfaction with the kind of petit
bourgeois life that his family had led in Stolp, and an increasing awareness of the
social injustices in German society. This awareness was itself probably fed partly by
his exposure to the effects of technical change in graphic reproduction, to the increasingly wide range of graphic work available in illustrated magazines, art jour-
nals, periodicals and newspapers, which were neither 'cartoons' nor 'caricatures',
but which were directly concerned with urban and social themes.

Many contemporary German graphic artists based in Berlin such as Käthe Kollwitz, Heinrich Zille and Hans Baluschek (Figures 8 and 9) were overtly preoccupied in their work with urban and working class problems, and with finding new
technical means or graphic styles through which to represent them. In Berlin,

1 Historical and artistic background

Figure 8 Käthe Kollwitz, Scenes of Poverty; 1909, *leaf 1,* Home Industry (Heimarbeit) *from* Simplicissimus, *Vol. 14, Nov. 15, 1909, p.515.*

Figure 9 Heinrich Zille, The Dark Berlin, *engraving. From* Jahrbuch der Jungen Kunst, *1920, No.27, p.113.*

Grosz seems to have become increasingly aware of the extent to which those forms of illustration that appeared in popular magazines and the escapist 'penny dreadfuls' could misrepresent reality, for after his arrival in Berlin he became preoccupied with everyday subjects which he observed around him, such as unemployment, workers on their way to work and the industrial suburbs (**Pls.IX.4, 6 and 7**).

At this time Grosz was beginning to consolidate his view that graphic art was an important medium in its own right – i.e. an *alternative* to, rather than a training for, 'high' art easel painting – and also that, through the development of new styles and techniques of reproduction, the medium could be used to produce an art which was accessible and relevant to contemporary social life. After the war years these views became more clearly formulated and expressed in his statements on *Tendenz-kunst* and the need for a 'proletarian art'.

On moving to Berlin, Grosz also became familiar with those modern European developments in easel painting which were featured, exhibited and sold through the Berlin art market.

In the years before the war the Berlin art market was particularly active. Private dealers such as Paul Cassirer, Schulte, and the Keller and Reiner gallery dealt in French and modern German works, helping to make Berlin into the art centre of Germany and Central Europe. By 1910 Paul Cassirer's gallery, founded with his brother Bruno in 1899, had established itself as Germany's leading gallery of modern French and German art. It held between six and eight annual shows. In the spring of 1904 Cassirer organized the first show of Cézannes in Germany; between 1907-8 the gallery held ten different exhibitions including Cézanne, Matisse and Munch. Cassirer's became a magnet for Central European buyers seeking French Impressionist and Post-Impressionist works, for even in Vienna at the time no individual dealer specialized in recent French art.

Cassirer's tastes and interests, not to mention his business sense, were immensely powerful within the Berlin art world. Apart from the success of his own gallery, and his art publishing company founded in 1908, he was closely associated with the Berlin Secession from its inception in 1898–9. In 1899 Paul and Bruno Cassirer became the Secession's managers (their official title was 'secretaries'), which gave them seats on the Secession's Executive Committee and 'advisory' votes. They also participated in the selection and hanging of exhibitions. In 1912 Cassirer was elected President of the Secession. The election was a controversial one and many members objected because Cassirer was not a practising artist, and – worse still – was a man of commerce. His status was therefore similar to that of the French dealers Durand-Ruel or Bernheim-Jeune who were discussed in earlier blocks on France. Several of those critics who favoured Cassirer's support of modern French and German art were in fact opposed to the election of a non-artist to the presidency; some hoped that the Secession would be run by 'creative' artists, who were driven by 'spiritual' forces as well as business acumen. Thus a contemporary critic, Julius Bab, discussed Cassirer's appointment as follows:

> To the extent that every association of artists is a group interested in effective exhibitions and good sales, the Secession will probably not fare badly under the knowledgeable and energetic leadership of Mr. Cassirer. But if we keep in mind that such a group should also be a social organization, the self-government of free, creative spirits, then some of us will not welcome the presidency of this layman. . . .
> (*Karlsruher Zeitung*, 11 December, 1912.)

This statement suggests that the 'Expressionist' concern (discussed in Block IV) with an art practice that is a separate spiritual activity supposedly removed from social and economic life, was a dominant attitude within avant-garde art circles in Berlin at this time.

When Grosz came to Berlin in 1912, the Berlin Secession exhibitions and the larger private galleries mainly determined his access to contemporary European art. It seems likely that he would have visited Cassirer's Secession show of 1913 which included a large number of foreign works, including those by Cézanne, Bonnard, Van Gogh, Renoir, Seurat, Derain, Vlaminck, Marquet, Friesz and Matisse (including *La Danse* of 1910). The German artists represented included the Brücke members Kirchner, Heckel, Schmidt-Rottluff and Pechstein, and Liebermann and Max Beckmann (see Television Programme 21). Julius Bab, who had previously had reservations about Cassirer's appointment, raved about the show in the *Karls-ruher Zeitung* (May 1913), proclaiming it a triumph of modern painting. Perhaps Bab had come to realize that the 'creative spirit' of a painter, which he believed was missing in Cassirer, was not a necessary force in the organization of a successful exhibition.

German supporters of Cassirer's patronage of modern European art also welcomed the opening of Herwarth Walden's Der Sturm (The Storm) gallery in March 1912. Walden had started a weekly magazine of the same name in 1910. The magazine, which published works by young writers, included prints and full-page woodcuts by artists such as Oscar Kokoschka (Figure 10) and the Brücke group.

Figure 10 Oskar Kokoschka,
Portrait of Herwarth Walden,
1910, black ink over graphite,
11½ in. x 8½ in. 29 cm x 22 cm.
Courtesy of the Fogg Art Museum,
Harvard University. Purchase –
Friends of Art and Music at
Harvard. © *S.P.A.D.E.M.,*
Paris, 1982.

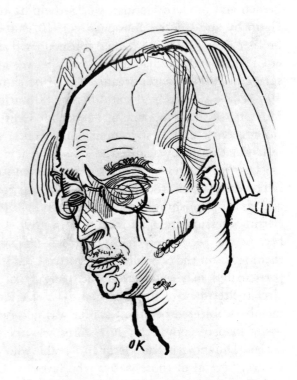

Walden's gallery opened in March with an exhibition of work by Blaue Reiter artists (see Radiovision Programme 14). From 10 April to 31 May he held an influential touring show of Italian Futurism (it had already been shown in Paris and London) which included works by Boccioni, Carrà, Russolo, and Severini (see Block VI). In addition Walden, who was an admirer of Marinetti, printed several Futurist manifestoes in *Der Sturm* magazine. Walden's determination to promote the Italian Futurists was further demonstrated by the fact that he persuaded his associate, the banker Dr. Borchardt, to buy 24 of the 29 pictures in the show.

Like Cassirer, Walden had a powerful influence on the interests and developments in the modern art market and tastes in Germany at the time. Grosz was a regular visitor to Der Sturm gallery, and was clearly influenced by the Italian exhibition. Many of his works from 1912 onwards used 'diagonal lines of force' and angular splintered designs (**Col.pls.IX.1, 3 and 12,** and Figure 11) reminiscent of Futurist works. And like the Futurists he often used these techniques to suggest dynamic movements of urban life in his paintings and drawings. However, it is dangerous to draw too close a parallel with the Futurists' fanatical adulation of the speed and technology of the city. Rather, Grosz had a sense of both its technological advances and its serious social problems.

In his section on *Art in Germany 1920–40*, Hamilton (p. 474) emphasizes Walden's importance in the Berlin art world and singles out what was called the 'First German *Salon d'Automne*' comparing it with Roger Fry's London exhibitions of 1910–12 'as one of the few occasions when one individual comprehended the fundamental directions of the modern movement'. In this exhibition Walden showed

360 German works alongside paintings by Chagall, Delaunay, Brancusi, Mondrian, Ernst, Arp and Archipenko. Hamilton assumes that individuals like Walden understand – or 'comprehend' – directions rather than interpret them. We have been trying to show above that Walden's selection and promotion of artists and groups for exhibitions helped to determine a German view of what constituted Modernism. To say that Walden somehow understood the direction of the modern movement suggests that there was a self-propelling movement that existed independently of its interpretations, exhibiting preferences and critical categorizations. The German view of the modern movement in 1912 was slightly different to, for example, the English view, shaped largely by the content of Fry's 'Post-Impressionist' exhibitions. And Hamilton's assessment of Walden could equally well be applied to Cassirer or Julius Meier-Graefe, who both made significant contributions to the German 'understanding' of modern art. As we saw in Block IV, Meier-Graefe was the first German critic to develop a theory of modern art based on contemporary French art, and outlined in his highly influential *Development of Modern Art* published in 1904.

Berlin and the First World War

Both Grosz's technical interests and his choice of themes were affected by developments and activities within the Berlin art world. But from 1914 his choice of subjects for drawings, most of which were personal sketches or executed for illustrated magazines, show him to be especially preoccupied with the effects of the war on everyday life in Berlin.

On 3 August 1914, Germany declared war on France. Although the political parties in the Reichstag (German parliament) originally agreed to a so-called political 'truce' in the interests of the war effort, as the war progressed and casualties escalated, increasing attacks were made on the Reichstag's pro-war policies, in particular its approval of war loans. (The events of the war are listed more fully in the historical chart reproduced as Appendix A.)

Grosz's pen and ink drawings such as his *Street Fight* of 1914 (**Pls.IX.8 and 9**) record some of the many Berlin street battles, often caused by political clashes, which accompanied the outbreak of war. His *Café Scene* of 1914 (**Pl.IX.10**) depicts another change in urban life: the large Berlin café restaurant, the Café Denis, is now full of soldiers, some sporting their injuries and iron crosses. In this work his figure drawing has a stiff linear quality, which was to become the hallmark of many of his post-war satirical drawings, and which is used here to accentuate the ugliness of his subjects, many of whom wear or display the symbols of war.

▶ Look at two more drawings by Grosz that represent Berlin street life during the early war years:

Riot of the Insane, 1915 (**Pl.IX.11**), and *Pandemonium*, 1914 (**Pl.IX.12**).

What image of Berlin society do these drawings suggest? In answering this you might consider the following questions: are any recognizable social activities represented here; can we identify any clear relationship between groups or classes of people; does any one group seem more oppressed than another? ◀

▷ In *Riot of the Insane*, contemporary life is depicted as a sequence of insane brawls, men fighting, raping of women, burning houses, a child hanging from a lamp-post and a pillaged church. Sailors, workers, women, the bowler-hatted middle classes and the church are all involved. As in *Pandemonium* the urban environment is characterized by symbols of death, depravity and horror.

Although both these drawings show a concern with the depiction of social turmoil and its effects, Grosz seems to make no distinction between exploiters and exploited. Clear references to the oppression of the working class, and the corruption of middle class figureheads, which recur in later drawings (**Pls.IX.3, 33 and 35**) are absent here. Bowler-hatted and suited men appear to be no less aggressive and vile than the swarthier, bare-armed figures. Even the thin down-trodden workers of some of his pre-war drawings are absent here (**Pls.IX.4, 6 and 7**). And the women in both drawings are frequently depicted as victims, usually of sexual attack, a preoccupation that we will be discussing in the section on the *Ecce Homo* portfolio.

Possible explanations for this confusing imagery can be found in some of Grosz's contemporary interests and statements. At this time Grosz, like many other German intellectuals, did not have clearly defined targets for radical attack. The beginning of the war tended to disrupt some pre-existing political alignments and attitudes in the interest of the combined war effort. Many artists of both the right and left became submerged in a 'war psychosis' (which we discuss in the following section) which Grosz quickly came to despise. A series of letters to his American friend Bob Bell, written during the second half of 1915 after Grosz had joined the army and been discharged, suggest that the early war experience had at first made him violently anti-German rather than actively political. A letter of 28 May attacks the current ideology of 'patriotism and corruption', claiming 'Germany shows her true face — a hopeless harlequinade'. And an undated letter from the same year fiercely criticizes those patriotic Germans:

> Day after day my hatred of the Germans is fuelled fresh to burning flames by the impossibly ugly, unaesthetic, badly dressed Germans. From an aesthetic point of view, I am happy about every German who dies a hero's death on the field of honour. To be a German means always to be ill-mannered, stupid, ugly, fat and to be the worst sort of reactionary – to be unwashed.
> (Reproduced in H. Hess, *George Grosz*, 1974, p.51.)

Although he professed vague socialist sympathies at the time, his more active participation in an organized political struggle did not take place until the end of the war when he joined the German Communist Party (KPD).

As a result of his anti-German feelings, Grosz developed an escapist craving for an idealized alternative culture of America. Like many contemporary Germans who were drawn into a cult of America largely through illustrated magazines, cowboy stories and silent movies, he romanticized American life, writing in 1918 to his friend Otto Schmalhausen of his passion for 'the fabulous civilization of steel construction and elastic grain elevators' (22 April, 1918). In *The Adventurer*, an oil painting (now lost) of 1916 (Figure 11), Grosz painted himself in American clothes, complete with cowboy hat, trousers, spurs, flick knife and a gun and liquor bottle hanging from his belt. In the same year he had considered emigrating, and as is suggested in *The Adventurer* he began to dress in American clothes. In 1916-17 he also signed drawings and letters with American pen names and changed his first name from the German Georg to George. And in his first portfolio or *Mappe*, the *Erste George Grosz-Mappe* of 1917, his concentration on the urban theme included New York subjects in which trains, tall buildings and skyscrapers jostle for space (**Pl.IX.13**). Although he felt distaste for the corruption and hypocrisy of urban life, he was attracted to the speed, the technology and the excitement of the modern city, echoing the preoccupations, though not the ideology, of the Italian Futurists, who had exhibited in Der Sturm gallery in Berlin in 1912. New York represented what he called the 'bouncing excitement' of the big cities (letter to Otto Schmalhausen, 30 June 1917).

Figure 11 George Grosz, The Adventurer, *1916, oil on canvas, whereabouts unknown. Photo from H. Hess,* George Grosz, *Studio Vista, London, 1974.* © S.P.A.D.E.M., Paris, 1982.

Grosz was called up again in January 1917, and by the time of his second discharge in April of that year, everyday life in Berlin had become increasingly difficult, thus fuelling his romantic yearning for an alternative life in America. The urban chaos that Grosz observed is recorded in graffiti-like sketches of Berlin at night, littered with graves or as the scene of endless social disturbances (Pls.IX.12,14,15 and 16). By 1917 Berlin, like the whole of Germany, had been severely hit by family deaths, poverty and food shortages. The cost of the war had been enormous, and it had been heavily financed by escalating war loans (see Appendix B) which had upset the German currency structure and caused massive cuts in government funds to needy areas of social support.

After his appointment to the supreme command in August 1916, Hindenburg announced the so-called Hindenburg Programme which set targets for the doubling of munitions production and the trebling of cannon and machine gun production by the spring of 1917. These measures, while increasing the demand for – and exploitation of – female labour in heavy industries, also caused increased fuel shortages, which directly affected the transportation of food, and involved the sacrifice of civic funds. The Allied naval blockade also caused acute food shortages and heavy rationing. Many starved in the streets of Berlin – in Germany as a whole it has been estimated (Schneede, p.141) that three-quarters of a million people died of starvation between 1914-18 – where public soup kitchens, food queues and the street riots so frequently recorded by Grosz, were a regular feature of everyday life.

In the social and economic climate of war-time Berlin there was little demand, nor the money available, for 'high' art canvases, and the art market stagnated. If Grosz was to make a living through art he was more likely to succeed by working in the cheaper and more accessible medium of graphic art. Magazines and newspapers continued to be published throughout the war, and it was through his contributions to anti-war publications such as *Die Aktion* that Grosz could publicize his own views on the war and its effects.

Artists' reactions to the First World War

By 1917 morale in most social and political circles in Germany was low. Early appeals to an instinct for heroism and for support for the 'great' *Vaterland* had lost their persuasive powers in view of the enormous numbers of dead and seriously injured German soldiers. Grosz described his own early disillusionment thus:

> When war was declared there was mass intoxication. I volunteered and became an infantryman assigned to a regiment that was sent to a quiet sector on the Western front. The initial frenzy and enthusiasm, however, were quickly dissipated, leaving nothing behind for most of us but a vast emptiness. The appeal of the gun and helmet soon wore off and war represented only the grim and the horrible. It came to mean filth, lice, idiocy, disease and deformity. Of course, there was some heroism. There were idealists who wanted to give their all for the Fatherland.
>
> (*A Little Yes and a Big No*, p. 145.)

In 1915 after six months' service Grosz was discharged on medical grounds and returned to Berlin, where he contributed drawings to the magazine *Die Aktion*. In January 1917 he was redrafted; the German generals had resolved to step up their offensives and new conscripts were necessary to replace the appalling casualties. Grosz's reaction, according to his letters from the time, was one of horror and profound insecurity. His 'nerves went to pieces' (letter to Otto Schmalhausen, 15 March 1917) and he was eventually put in a psychiatric hospital near Brandenburg, to be discharged three months later.

In 1914, however, Grosz seems to have viewed the war more optimistically, although the precise nature of his early attitudes towards war have been interpreted differently by different biographers (Hans Hess, for example, plays down Grosz's early enthusiasm, arguing that he volunteered to improve his opportunities within the army.) In 1914 Grosz believed that:

> War will not only rekindle repressed instincts which lie dormant inside us all, but also truly liberate many people – whether from a hated environment, from the slavery of the daily grind or from the burden of their own personality.
>
> (Quoted in U. Schneede, *George Grosz – His Life and Work*, p. 30.)

These kinds of early expectations were common among artists and writers who otherwise had no political support for the Kaiser's régime. War was greeted with enthusiasm for different and seemingly incompatible reasons. Many writers saw it as a source of a hoped-for spiritual rejuvenation, while others supported it as a symbol of German militarist policies. The historian Peter Gay has described a 'war psychosis' in the West. In Block VI you saw how the Italian Futurists greeted war with a similar enthusiasm as a form of spiritual cleansing. Gay argues that in Germany 'this psychosis reached the heights of absurdity. The over-aged, the adolescent, the unfit volunteered with pure joy, and went to death filled with their mission'. He goes on to quote the words of the writers Thomas Mann and Friedrich Gundolf:

> The war offered 'purification, liberation, and enormous hope'; it 'set the hearts of poets aflame' with a sense of relief that 'a peaceful world had collapsed', a world of which 'one was so tired, so dreadfully tired'. Only 'victory at any price' could give life meaning; the Germans had at last united as a *Volk*, Germans alone were 'truthful, authentic, manly, objective', a land of heroes facing opponents saddled with 'cowardice, mendacity and baseness', grand old words like *Volk* and *Reich* and *Geist* were now given new meaning by this great crusade for *Kultur*.
>
> (*Weimar Culture*, p. 12.)

You should recall from Block IV that a preoccupation with the notion of an idealized German *Volk* had dominated a good deal of cultural criticism around the turn of the century. By 1918 the narrower concept of *Volk* (in the sense of the indigenous German peasantry) had broadened, with many seeing in war – as Gay suggests – a chance for Germans to revive and reassert a nationalist identity as a united *Volk* with strong spiritual roots.

Some of Gay's assumptions are justified by the attitudes of many German painters. Many of the artists associated with relatively progressive exhibiting groups such as the Berlin Secession supported Germany's entry into the war. Lovis Corinth (**Pls.IV.47 and 48**), who was then one of the best-known painters in Germany, wrote an essay entitled *Vae Victis*, in which he praised the 'teutonic will' which 'showed the enemy that he could not disturb our peaceful existence with impunity'. Another important member of the Berlin Secession, Max Liebermann, put his name to the 'Declaration of the Ninety-Three', a declaration signed by writers, scientists, academics and artists which patriotically defended Germany against the charge of aggression. Many Expressionist artists joined up on the outbreak of war, seeing it in terms similar to those of Thomas Mann and Friedrich Gundolf, as a purifying storm and a chance to rebuild society. Erich Heckel and Max Beckmann both volunteered for the medical corps, and the latter's *War Letters*, written during 1914, show an initial excitement – enjoyment even – for the war.

There were very few publications that openly opposed the war at the beginning; one that did was the magazine *Die Aktion*, founded in 1911 by Franz Pfemfert. *Die Aktion* published drawings, poems and articles critical of the war and the attitudes of those who supported it. Those writers and journalists who fed the war propaganda machine were a major target, the same writers to whom Grosz refers in a letter of 1915: 'The time is favourable for charlatans . . . from meat substitute manufacturers to courtly lyric poets, those prisoners of war' (quoted in H. Hess, *George Grosz*, p. 51). In 1915 *Die Aktion* published a poem and drawings by Grosz and he soon became a regular contributor to the magazine, thus clearly establishing himself as an anti-war artist.

In the same year Grosz met the young writer Wieland Herzfelde, who was planning to found another anti-war magazine, to be called *Die Neue Jugend*, a title taken from a schoolboys' magazine. Grosz was introduced to Wieland's brother Helmut Herzfelde, the painter and graphic designer who changed his name to John Heartfield (Heartfield's work is discussed in Radiovision Programme 20) and both Wieland and Helmut were impressed with Grosz's drawings, seeing *Die Neue Jugend* as a major vehicle for the dissemination of Grosz's work. The first issue appeared in July 1916, and included two of Grosz's drawings, one of which is reproduced as **Pl.IX.17**. In the following year the April edition was banned. *Die Neue Jugend*, from which the Malik Verlag (Malik Publishing House) was founded in 1917, played an important role in the early publication and publicizing of Grosz's work.

▶ Look at Grosz's drawing, *Stick It Out*, 1915 (**Pl.IX.17**), which appeared in the first edition of *Die Neue Jugend* in 1916, and two other drawings in which Grosz treats war themes:

The Shell, 1915 (**Pl.IX.18**) executed during his first period of military service; and *'K.V.' Fit for Active Service*, 1916-17 (**Pl.IX.19**), published in the *God is on our Side* portfolio in 1920 by Malik Verlag, where it was entitled *The Faith Healers*.

Each of these drawings is based on the theme of war. Bearing in mind the information provided on the preceding pages about Grosz's attitudes towards the war, and the contexts in which these drawings were produced and published, would you describe any – or all – of these as anti-war drawings? Why would you use this label? ◀

▷ Clearly, there is no one right or wrong answer to the first part of this question, because a reading of these – or each of these – works as 'anti-war' will depend on a number of variable factors which include the contexts in which they were produced and consumed, the intentions of the artist at the time of executing the drawing, the nature of the publication (if relevant) for which the drawing was produced, the types of formal conventions used and the associations that those would have had for a contemporary audience.

That said, we know that Grosz executed *The Shell* while on military service, when (as we have seen) he was horrified by the carnage and waste that he saw around him. But there is a difference between the interpretation of the subject in *The Shell* and the other two drawings. *The Shell* is a sketchy pen and ink drawing, showing bodies and corpses thrown out by the explosion. It is a record of a war activity and because it selects an unpleasant event as its subject it could be seen as a protest against war; the frightening image does not seek to idealize or glorify events. *Fit for Active Service*, on the other hand, is making a clearer satirical point. In this, Grosz distorts and exaggerates physical features and idiosyncrasies and is clearly being ironic when the medical officer pronounces a skeleton 'K.V.' or fit for service. In this work, as in *Stick It Out*, the title gives it a satirical edge that is lacking in the straightforward title *The Shell*. And the coffins which dominate the scene of *Stick It Out* also assume an ironic function in relation to the title.

It seems, then, that Grosz intended each of these to be understood as anti-war drawings, although this is more clearly read out of the two works which use satire and caricature. And the contexts in which they appeared and the commitments of those who consumed them made a difference to the ways in which such works were received. Those drawings which, like *The Shell*, were not obviously satirical were more likely to be received as protest pictures if published in an anti-war magazine such as *Die Aktion* or *Die Neue Jugend*, where they would have been consumed and interpreted by pacifist readers. ◁

Political repercussions of the war and the formation of the Weimar Republic

As war progressed Grosz, as we shall see, came increasingly to identify his own 'anti-war' attitudes with a specific left-wing party political position. His interests and activities, like those of many German artists, were at least partly shaped by social and political developments in contemporary Germany. These developments, which are described very briefly below, helped to generate some of the dominant political debates on the function and nature of 'socialism' and 'communism' as political forces in post-war Germany.

By 1917 political opposition to the war and the Kaiser's government was strengthening. The Russian Revolution of March 1917 changed the political and military structure of Europe. It was seen by the government as a warning signal, necessitating some domestic constitutional reforms, and by the left as a political encouragement. The German socialist movement, which had been united before the war, was divided in April 1917 into two parties. The Independent Social Democratic Party of Germany (USPD) formed a breakaway parliamentary group asserting its opposition to war and its ideological independence from the Social Democratic Party (SPD). In the same year the USPD was joined by the Spartacus group, led by Karl Liebknecht and Rosa Luxemburg, which had broken away from the SPD in 1914. The Spartacists were internationalist in outlook and, according to their founding manifesto, were committed to the 'international class struggle against the war so that peace could be enforced through the will of the masses'.

By September 1918 the war seemed to be lost for Germany (see Appendix A). But on 28 October the German navy planned yet another offensive against the English, which resulted in a naval mutiny. The mutiny was soon supported at Kiel by workers and soldiers demanding an end to the war, the release of political prisoners and imprisoned seamen, a free press and universal suffrage. Influenced by the example of the Bolshevik revolution, workers', and soldiers' councils were formed throughout Germany in support of these demands, events which have been called the 'November Revolution'. Kaiser Wilhelm II abdicated on 9 November and on the same day the office of Reichs Chancellor was transferred from Crown Prince Max of Baden to Friedrich Ebert, President of the SPD. The war was over and the Weimar Republic was officially established.

On the same day Karl Liebknecht of the USPD proclaimed a 'Socialist Republic'. He and his followers demanded complete reform of the army, reduced working hours, a fixed minimum wage, expropriation of all funds owned by banks and control of the mines and the steel industry. Ebert won over many USPD members by offering concessions; these allowed the Berlin Soldiers' and Workers' Councils provisional power until the constituent parliament met. A National Assembly at Weimar was elected in January 1919, by which time Ebert had made a pact with the military, thus aggravating the tension with many members of the USPD.

The winter of 1918-19 was torn by political strife, the effects of which influenced Grosz's political and artistic activities. In December the Spartacists, disillusioned with the events of the November Revolution, split from the USPD to form the German Communist Party (KPD) (Figure 12), and attempted an insurrection

Figure 12 Poster for the KPD (Spartacus), 1918. Preussischer Kulturbesitz, Bildarchiv.

by taking over many of Berlin's public buildings. On 14 December an article by Rosa Luxemburg in the communist newspaper, *Die Rote Fahne* (*The Red Flag*), set out the aims of the Spartacist group. This article became the founding manifesto of the KPD on 31 December, and in its wake the establishment and right-wing organizations accelerated anti-communist propaganda campaigns in posters and advertisements. Right-wing organizations warned the German people against a bolshevik/Jewish/Spartacist conspiracy that would take over and destroy German society

(Figure 2) while the SPD appealed to workers and soldiers to ignore the 'bolshevism' of the Spartacists which would turn Germany into another Russia (Figure 1). To counter the activities of the KPD the Social Democrats also recruited the notorious *Freikorps*, a para-military organization consisting mainly of ex-officers and freebooters. The insurrection of 31 December was put down, and Rosa Luxemburg and Karl Liebknecht were both arrested and murdered as they emerged from their hiding place on 15 January 1919. And a month later the Bavarian USPD leader Karl Eisner was murdered in Munich. Both incidents, which were much publicized in the press, increased the atmosphere of disillusionment and suspicion among working people and the political left, and exacerbated anti-government feeling among intellectuals.

Many artists, including Grosz and Käthe Kollwitz, saw and represented the Luxemburg/ Liebknecht murders as a symbol of oppression by the military and the government (often called 'the White Terror') in the post-war years. In Grosz's *Remember 1919* (**Pl.IX.20**) an executioner in a black robe and trailing blood, a symbol of the White Terror, moves over the Spartacists' coffins. Käthe Kollwitz uses the harsh black-and-white lines of the woodcut to emphasize the sorrow and mourning of workers around Liebknecht's tomb in *In Memory of Karl Liebknecht* (Figure 13). These works were clearly intended and would have been read as political symbols. Contemporary statistics provide some relevant background. According

Figure 13 Käthe Kollwitz, In Memory of Karl Liebknecht, *1919–1920, woodcut.*
Philadelphia Museum of Art.

to public records, between 1918 and 1922 twenty-two assassinations were traced to left-wing elements and seventeen of these were severely punished, ten with the death penalty. Assassinations by the right wing numbered 354, but only one of these was severely punished and did not receive the death penalty.

Despite these developments, the early events of the November 'Revolution' had been greeted enthusiastically by artists and intellectuals disillusioned with the Kaiser's régime and the slaughter of war. We have seen in the Introduction that Grosz was among a group of such artists who joined the *Novembergruppe*, established in 1918. The group included architects, artists and sculptors committed (according

Figure 14 Max Pechstein, title page of November-gruppe Guidelines (An Alle Künstler*), 1919. Photo from R. Hamann and J. Hermand,* Expressionismus, *Akademie-Verlag, Berlin, 1977, p.234.*

Figure 15 César Klein, The New Phoenix, *1919. Photo from R. Hamann and J. Hermand, op. cit., p.249*

to their 'Guidelines') 'to bring together radical artists' (Figure 14). Its founder members included the painters Otto Dix (**Pls. IX.21 and 22**), Rudolf Schlichter, (**Pl. IX.23**) César Klein (Figure 15) and Max Pechstein (Figures 14 and 20), and the architect Eric Mendelsohn. It was joined in December by the artists Otto Müller, Heinrich Campendonck and Hans Purrmann. At the beginning of 1919 a related organization, the *Arbeitsrat für Kunst* (Workers' Council for Art) was established. This 'Council' is discussed briefly in Hamilton (p.474). It was dominated by architects such as Otto Bartnung, Bruno Taut and Walter Gropius who went on to form the Weimar Bauhaus. The *Arbeitsrat* drew up ambitious plans, including Bartnung's scheme to abolish professorships in art and crafts schools, returning to a medieval master–apprenticeship relationship. Gropius had plans for a 'peoples' architecture', but this, like most *Arbeitsrat* schemes, never got beyond the drawing-board stage because of a post-war cessation of building.

While both these artists' groups officially supported the workers' and soldiers' councils and their demands, they had no political power and little direct contact with politically active groups. By 1920 the *Novembergruppe* had become little more than an exhibiting group (the *Novembergruppe* exhibitions are mentioned in Hamilton, p.474) because members held divergent views on politics and the function of art within society. The work and attitudes of those artists who had become established 'Expressionists', such as Max Pechstein and César Klein (Figures 14, 15 and 20), were increasingly opposed by those artists (including Grosz) who were more concerned with using art to achieve 'revolutionary' left-wing goals, and who worked in so-called 'realist' styles. This second group formed the core of the left-wing opposition within the *Novembergruppe*, whose protest letter of 1921, published in *Der Gegner* (*Supplementary Documents*, IX. 4), was discussed in the Introduction. Many members of the opposition group, such as Grosz, Otto Dix, Raoul Hausmann, Hannah Höch, Rudolf Schlichter and Georg Scholz (**Pl.IX.24**), were associated with the Berlin Dada movement, whose more radical political concerns (see Radiovision Programme 19) had encouraged them to challenge the *Novembergruppe's* lack of commitment to its early aims.

The open letter in *Der Gegner* was one of many published statements to which Grosz contributed in the years 1920–21, and which set out his belief that the artist must actively participate in a political class struggle. He was one of several artists and intellectuals, including the publisher Wieland Herzfelde, his brother John Heartfield and the theatre director Erwin Piscator, who had become founder members of the KPD on 31 December 1918.

The KPD was one of many political parties formed during the immediate postwar years. In the 1920 Reichstag elections there were no less than sixteen main parties, of which ten received enough votes to give them at least one parliamentary seat. The chart (reproduced as Appendix D) lists these main parties and the number of seats won by each. You will see that the ruling SPD won by far the largest proportion of seats (113), the USPD being the nearest contender with 81 seats. The chart also tells us that while the left-wing KPD only had two seats, the two right-wing nationalist parties (DNVP and DVP) polled 66 and 62 seats respectively. The far right, then, was in a position to wield more direct political power than the far left, a fact that probably increased the demand within the KPD for the production and dissemination of an effective propagandist art through channels such as periodicals, magazines, newspapers and posters.

The need for left-wing artists to be overtly propagandist in their work is constantly reiterated in Grosz's written statements from this period. In *Art is in Danger*, a collection of articles written between 1920-25 and published in 1925, Grosz and Herzfelde summarized their belief that art must always reflect an ideological interest:

> There are still artists who deliberately and consciously attempt to avoid all tendentiousness (*Tendenzkunst*) remaining silent in the face of social events, not taking part, not accepting responsibility. As far as art is practised for its own sake, it propagates a blasé indifference and irresponsible individualism. The artist cannot withdraw himself from the laws of social development – today the class struggle. A detached stance, above or on the side lines, still means taking sides. Such indifference, and otherworldliness supports automatically the class in power – in Germany its bourgeoisie. . . .
> (G. Grosz and W. Herzfelde, *Art is in Danger*, 1925.)

Grosz and Herzfelde were arguing for political agitation through art, which is opposed to what they call 'pure art'. The concept of 'pure art' or 'art for art's sake' has preoccupied many Modernist artists who have concerned themselves with formal means which are seen as autonomous with respect to contemporary events. Those artists who, as we saw in the Introduction to this block, defended 'spiritual values' attacked the work of artists such as Grosz on the grounds that it was compromised by and contingent upon a political position. The left-wing artists' riposte was that the concept of enduring spiritual values was itself a product of the ideology of a specific historical class, namely the bourgeoisie.

Grosz and Russian Constructivism

The constant debating of such ideas within left-wing artistic and literary circles in Germany at the time encouraged many German artists to follow closely the political and artistic developments in Russia around 1920. In the preceding block, you studied the various artistic debates and activities which took place in post-revolutionary Russia, through which different groups of artists sought to resolve the problem of finding an appropriate art form to convey a political meaning. Access to Russian sources was subject to geographical, and in some cases political, restrictions, but the Berlin Dada group (see Radiovision Programme 19), with which Grosz was associated after the war, showed a special interest in some Russian Constructivist ideas and techniques. This is indicated by some of Grosz's pictures from 1920, in which figures and objects have mechanical or geometric forms (**Pls.IX.2 and 25**). In Part 3 we will consider Grosz's 1920 essay, *My New Pictures* (*Supplementary Documents*, IX.5), in which Grosz argues that the style of these works embodies revolutionary ideals. A revised version of this article was published in Mayakovsky's Soviet journal *Lef* in 1923, although Grosz himself soon became dissatisfied with this 'mechanical' style. A similar dissatisfaction with Constructivist styles was demonstrated in his negative reactions to the large Soviet Art Exhibition held in Berlin in 1922 which featured many Constructivist and Suprematist works, and which reflected a peculiarly German view of what the Russians were doing. This exhibition, and the view that it represented, are discussed in detail by Christina Lodder in Television Programme 18. In her biography of Grosz, Irwin Lewis has suggested that the change in Grosz's attitude may have been a reaction to Lenin's condemnation of Constructivism, but Grosz is also reported to have been horrified by Malevich's *White on White* (B. Irwin Lewis, *George Grosz — Art and Politics in the Weimar Republic*, p.100), presumably because of the Suprematist concern with 'pure' formal values that it was seen to embody. There was much artistic exchange and traffic between Russia and Berlin around 1922, although many of those Russian artists who emigrated to Germany, such as Kandinsky (who went to the Bauhaus), Pevsner and Gabo, represented more formalist concerns than the utilitarian 'Constructivist' interests which came to dominate *Inkhuk* and which were discussed in Block VIII.

Grosz, like many radical German artists, actively supported groups working for famine relief in Russia. He was one of many artists (including Otto Dix and Käthe Kollwitz) who designed posters for the International Workers' Aid (IAH) in Berlin. In 1922 he spent five months in Russia, where he met several political figures and artists, including Lenin and Vladimir Tatlin. Most reports (including his own retrospective comments) suggest that Grosz returned disillusioned with Soviet developments, although it may be inaccurate to claim — as some monographs have done — that this visit marked any clear change in his political views. For several years after the visit he kept up his association with German communist groups such as the KPD and as we shall see continued to be concerned with Marxist issues in his writings and in some aspects of his painted and graphic work.

When Grosz's written ideas on the necessary political function of art, such as those discussed above in the quotation from *Art is in Danger*, are related to the range of his own work between about 1918–25, we are again confronted with the problem of what forms of art actually constitute a political or propagandist art.

In 1920 he experimented with the 'mechanical' style of painting (**Pls.IX.2 and 25**) mentioned earlier, and at the same time many of his paintings used (as we shall see) formal conventions that are more closely associated with the Expressionist artists he criticized. His extensive use of the graphic medium was an important factor in his attempt to produce a genuinely 'political' art, but there are graphic works by Grosz from this period that are more overtly propagandist than others;

some of these works make quite specific references to political groups or events, such as *Remember 1919* (in memory of Rosa Luxemburg and Karl Liebknecht) (**Pl.IX.20**), or satirical drawings of Chancellor Ebert such as the cover of *Die Pleite*, No.7, 1923 (Figure 16). Other drawings concern themselves with broader social themes such as the German middle class family, as in *Teutonic Day*, 1921, from *Ecce Homo* (**Pl.IX.26**).

Figure 16 George Grosz, 'S.M.' – Reichs Chancellor Ebert; cover of the magazine Die Pleite, *No. 7, 1923. Photo from U. Schneede,* George Grosz – His Life and Work, *Gordon Fraser, London, 1979, p.71. © S.P.A.D.E.M., Paris, 1982.*

In his painted and graphic work from this period Grosz sought to maintain a relationship with the European avant-garde, while also producing overtly satirical and propagandist works that could be read in terms of their intended 'political' content. In Part 2 we will consider the problem of whether or not Grosz did – or could – successfully reconcile these aspects in his work.

2 Grosz and Weimar 1918–28

In his greatness and his narrowness, in his success and in his tragic fate, he was a profoundly divided personality: as a savage denigrator who harboured a secret love, who yearned for the bourgeois life that he despised and castigated, who consequently despised and castigated himself, and who nevertheless shrugged off his yearning with a smile . . ..

(W. Schmied – reference below.)

This quotation is taken from the introductory paragraph of the section on Grosz in the 1979 Arts Council exhibition catalogue: *Neue Sachlichkeit and German Realism of the Twenties*. It is intended to give us an enticing preliminary summary of Grosz as a 'tragic' and successful artist, whose work and attitudes are full of contradictions. But it is a rather glib art historical statement (of which there are many similar examples in monographs and articles on Grosz) which, even in the context of the subsequent essay, does not really help our understanding of Grosz's work and its relationship to his writings. We need to know what Schmied assumes as his criteria of 'greatness' and 'narrowness'. Is 'narrowness' a reference to Grosz's post-war communism? His apparent 'tragic fate' is equally ambiguous. The events of the artist's life might be interpreted differently by a writer who emphasized Grosz's *success* in Germany and America and the financial security which it brought him.

There are many aspects of Grosz's work and activities during the Weimar period that have confused art historians, and the notion of a 'divided personality' is one which appears in several monographs. Schmied's subsequent explanation that Grosz yearned for the very bourgeois life which he satirized is a general statement that presents us with an a-historical summary of Grosz's interests. It does not allow for the shifts in his theoretical and political interests and the changing historical circumstances to which these may be related. We have seen that he joined the KPD immediately after the war and many of his recorded statements from that time echo this political commitment, which he hoped to convey through his satirical drawings, prints and paintings. The easing off of his conscious political commitment becomes evident in the late 1920s when he left the KPD and became increasingly preoccupied with the idea of a new life in America.

Reasons for the recurrence of critical accounts that summarize the whole range of Grosz's work and attitudes in terms of a 'divided personality' can be found in his own writings. In many of his letters from 1913-15 to his friend Robert Bell, Grosz writes self-consciously of his yearnings for the very bourgeois life of which he was critical. In July 1913 he wrote:

My second ego is grunting with pleasure (one of the many second, third, fourth, etc. egos that dwell inside me) . . .. I am sitting in an intensely sap-green velvet armchair . . . in my hand a large glass of raspberry-coloured strawberry punch . . . at my head a bolster with tassles . . .. They are mostly made by elderly maiden ladies still waiting for their life; that is why, so people say, they have incorporated in their handwork some little conservative spirit of resignation: for the bolster is said to be an efficient deflector of accesses [*sic*] of democratic or even anarchistic ideas of any kind, which explains its popularity in conservative middle-class circles.

(Quoted in U. Schneede, *op.cit.*, p. 20.)

In another letter of 1915 to Robert Bell, Grosz describes being alone with his 'doubles', fantasy figures who include an aristocrat and an American doctor (Schneede, p.42). But his early preoccupations with fantasy 'doubles' and weaknesses for bourgeois comforts are not the same as the politically 'divided personality' implied in Schmied's quotation, and they precede Grosz's period of active political commitment. Another source of these ideas is Grosz's autobiography, written in 1946, in which he describes his work from the immediate post-war period:

> All these objects, people and events, I drew most carefully. I loved none of them, neither those in the restaurant nor the ones in the street. I was arrogant enough to call myself a natural scientist, not a painter nor, heaven forbid, a satirist. But in reality I myself was everybody I drew, the rich man favoured by fate, stuffing himself and guzzling champagne, as much as the one who stood outside in the pouring rain holding out his hand. I was, as it were, divided in two.
>
> (*A Little Yes and a Big No*, p. 121.)

Retrospective accounts by artists or art critics which attempt to rationalize and/or psychoanalyse earlier developments sometimes provide less useful explanations of works than statements made by artists at the time that they were producing the works in question. Grosz's autobiography was written in America in 1946 at a time when his views about society and the role of art had changed dramatically from those of around 1920. This should be borne in mind when we look for explanations of illustrations from the immediate post-war period in writings and statements made much later in his life, although we may be able to filter through the information, sorting out the factual evidence from the more speculative ideas.

Some of these points should become clearer in our discussions of specific works from the post-war period when Grosz executed many oil paintings and drawings of contemporary urban scenes. Look at a reproduction of one of these paintings (**Col.pl.IX.1**), and read the following statements, one by Grosz written at the time he painted the canvas, and one by the American critic Thomas Craven, from 1934:

1   At present I am busy painting a large picture of hell – gin alley of grotesque dead bodies and madmen, lots going on there – on a coffin at right angles Old Nick is riding across the picture, exiting to the left, on the right a young man is spewing up all the beautiful illusions of youth onto the canvas – it is to Oscar Panizza that I have dedicated this picture. A teeming throng of possessed human animals – I am unshaken in my view that this epoch is sailing down to its destruction our soiled paradise . . . think that wherever you step, there's the smell of shit.

   (Letter to Otto Schmalhausen, 15 December 1917.)

2   During this dark period, a curious Futurist mania was at work in his art. His drawings were kaleidoscopic scraps – murderous in implication, his huge paintings (including *Oscar Panizza*) were symbolical confusions; forms seen through forms; soldiers, priests, pedagogues, judges, prostitutes, thieves, beggars and plutocrats, truncated and distributed among filth and falling buildings, the idea being to reveal simultaneously the actors, the scene and all the dismal wreckage of the chaotic Fatherland. Aesthetes prefer the work of this period, prating in their own lingo of the ectoplasmic vision, dynamic organization and plastic purity.

   (T. Craven, 'George Grosz' in *Modern Art*, p. 212.)

   (*Note:* Oscar Panizza was a psychiatrist and writer who had been tried twice (once for blasphemy and then for *lèse majesté*) for his satirical comments. From 1904 he had been committed to a mental hospital. Grosz's own sojourn in a mental institution helped him to view Panizza with great sympathy.)

▶ After reading the two quotations and relating them to the illustration, how would you decide which pieces of information were more helpful in interpreting this painting in its historical context? What kinds of information about the techniques used are provided in Craven's quotation? ◀

▷ The first paragraph, written while Grosz was working on the painting, is useful in helping us to understand and sort out the subject matter. A skeletal figure of death is riding across the picture, and Grosz clearly intended the work to present a grotesque image of destruction, disillusionment and humanity gone mad. (In a later account of 1930 he explained that the dehumanized figures represented alchohol, syphilis, and pestilence.) As it was written in 1917, we can reasonably assume that this account directly conveys his intentions and his feelings of disillusionment at the end of the war.

Craven's passage is concerned with the painting as one of a group and is therefore less specific in its information. His account is concerned primarily with the strange 'Futurist mania' and (though he mentions it with irony) 'dynamic organization'. Although Craven's final and rather pretentious sentence suggests that he is scathing of those critics who are preoccupied with the formal content of these paintings, his own account is primarily concerned with the formal organization, with 'forms seen through forms'. A more useful account of this series of paintings might give us more information on what the works signified in their historical context and why Grosz chose to represent these images in this way. As we shall see in Part 3, Craven's approach to Grosz is typical of many American critics writing after the Second World War who have seen Grosz's work as an interesting digression within the history of Modernism.

This is not to say that the technical aspects of this work are not important, but rather that they cannot be dissociated from other artistic and historical material. In this painting there is not just a 'Futurist mania' at work. The strong diagonal rhythms and the chaotic, crowded concentration of figures were conventions used by many contemporary German Expressionist artists such as Franz Marc (Col.pl.VI.12), Ludwig Meidner, César Klein or Max Pechstein (Figures 14, 15 and 20). Splintered diagonal rhythms, suggesting an almost apocalyptic explosion, were used by a wide range of Expressionist painters and illustrators, often to evoke different sorts of meanings. For example, the pantheistic undertones of Marc's *Fate of the Animals* (Col.pl.VI.12) discussed in Television Programme 14 are very different from the idealistic call for 'artistic freedom' symbolized by Klein's print of a phoenix rising from the flames in Figure 15. In *Oscar Panizza*, on the other hand, Grosz has used similar conventions to suggest a contemporary image of social destruction and depravity. The organization of the work is very similar to that of Grosz's graphic works from the war period, such as *Pandemonium*, 1914 (Pl.IX.12), but as an easel painting it has been more easily accommodated within Modernist histories of art. This is partly because there are parallels to be drawn with the techniques of Futurism and German Expressionism, but also because as Craven himself implies, it's much easier to apply concepts like 'plastic purity' when the work is painted in rich areas of bright colour, rather than drawn in the graffiti-like pencil or pen and ink style of much of Grosz's graphic work from this period. ◁

Drawings from the early twenties: illustrated magazines and newspapers

Grosz is probably better known for his graphic work, especially his satirical drawings that appeared in illustrated periodicals, magazines and portfolios during the Weimar period.

Newspaper and periodical production in Germany had accelerated dramatically between unification of the country in 1871 and the outbreak of the First World War, increasing the opportunities for a large number of graphic artists and illustrators. The rapid urbanization and introduction of universal education which followed unification increased the demand for and the production of newspapers. In 1866 there were approximately 1,500 newspapers in circulation (of which only 300 appeared daily) compared with about 3,500 in 1900. By 1914 this had increased to 4,200 of which approximately half appeared daily. Technical advances in printing also facilitated and increased the production of illustrated newspapers, such as the *Leipziger Illustrierte Zeitung* (similar to the *Illustrated London News*) and illustrated supplements, such as *Ulk*, the satirical weekly supplement of the liberal paper *Berliner Tageblatt*, to which Grosz contributed his first published drawing (Figure 5).

The extent of German newspaper production is underlined by a comparison with Britain, where newspapers numbered about 2,400 in 1914. Regional dispersion, reflecting local religious and cultural allegiances from before unification, was a characteristic of the German press. M. Eksteins, in *The Limits of Reason* (1975), has estimated that the 41 German cities with populations exceeding 100,000 averaged about 15 local papers each. Although not on the same scale, a similar decentralization can be found in the production of literary and art periodicals. In the 1890s, Munich became the centre for publishing *Jugendstil* periodicals such as *Jugend, Pan* and *Simplicissimus*, all founded between 1895–6.

However, Berlin soon became the centre for the publication of 'Expressionist' magazines. Many of these magazines, modelled on Walden's *Der Sturm*, included literature, poetry and graphics. In the immediate post-war period there was a dramatic increase in the production of magazines of this kind, an increase which was partly inspired by post-war ideals of creating a new society with new artistic freedoms (ideals epitomized in the *Novembergruppe* 'Guidelines', *Supplementary Documents*, IX.2). However, as cynicism and disillusionment set in with the early events of the Weimar Republic, these periodicals went out of circulation as quickly as they had appeared. This post-war rise and fall of 'Expressionist' magazines is recorded by John Willett below (Figure 17):

Year	At Beginning	At End
1917	7	10
1918	15	23
1919	35	44
1920	36	22
1921	?	15
1922	?	8

Figure 17 Post-war rise and fall of 'Expressionist' magazines. From J. Willett, Expressionism, *Weidenfeld and Nicholson. 1970, p.133.*

This information helps us to put Grosz's activities and interests in a clearer perspective. As we have seen, Grosz realized at an early age that he could make a living from 'caricatures' and increased opportunities for illustrators and graphic artists accompanied the accelerated production of illustrated newspapers and magazines in 1900–1920.

This may be one reason why so many contemporary German artists worked extensively — or almost exclusively — in the graphic medium. When Grosz came to Berlin and began to work as a freelance illustrator he would have become familiar with a wide range of graphic work in periodicals, art magazines and portfolios, which had little in common with the illustrations in the 'penny dreadfuls'.

Many so-called German 'Expressionist' artists had worked extensively in the graphic medium. You saw in Block IV that prints and woodcuts were important for the Brücke group of artists, and many 'Expressionist' artists working after the war, particularly those associated with the *Novembergruppe*, made extensive use of the print medium. These included Klein, Feininger (Figure 18), Conrad Felixmüller (Figure 19), and Pechstein (Figure 20), whose work would have been known to

Figure 18 Lyonel Feininger, Buttelstedt, *woodcut, published in* Jahrbuch der Jungen Kunst, *1920, No. 27, p.204.*

Figure 19 Conrad Felixmüller, In Memory of Karl Liebknecht and Rosa Luxemburg, *1919. Photo from R. Hamann and J. Hermand*, op. cit., *p.258.*

Figure 20 Max Pechstein, Talking, *1917, woodcut. Photo from R. Hamann and J. Hermand*, op. cit., *p.56.* ⓒ *S.P.A.D.E.M., Paris 1982.*

Grosz. And we have already mentioned the graphic work of Berlin-based artists such as Kollwitz, Baluschek and Zille, whose images of contemporary urban life may have helped to influence Grosz's own choice of techniques and themes. In the 1920s, the prints of Franz Masereel who worked extensively in the woodcut medium, impressed Grosz. After a trip in 1924 to Paris, where Masereel was then working, Grosz expressed his enthusiasm for Masereel's work, writing that he 'distinguishes himself from other painters in Paris, by not painting guitars' (Hess, pp. 126–27). At the time Masereel was working on a woodcut series of the city. The themes of the modern city, urban corruption and crowded scenes recurred in his work, as in his 'novel' in pictures, *Passionate Journey (Die Passion eines Menschen)* 1921 (Figure 21). Like Grosz, Masereel was a socialist, although his imagery often presented more sentimental, optimistic images of contemporary society than those that predominated in Grosz's prints and drawings of urban life from around 1920.

Figure 21 Franz Masereel, woodcut from 'Die Passion eines Menschen', *1921. Photo from R. Hamann and J. Hermand*, op. cit., *p.236.*

What exactly were Grosz's graphic interests immediately after the war? In 1918, he became closely associated with the Malik Verlag, the publishing company run by his close friend Wieland Herzfelde. With Herzfelde and John Heartfield he was a founder of the satirical magazines *Die Pleite (Gone Bust,* or *Bankruptcy)* and *Der blutige Ernst (Deadly Earnest)* with Carl Einstein. Both magazines were first published by Malik in 1919. Grosz was responsible for many of the first covers of *Die Pleite* (Pls.IX. 1, 27 and Figure 16). On the second issue (drawn when, according to Count Kessler's diaries (see Further Reading List), 'Grosz professed himself to be a Spartacist') he attacks Noske, the Social Democrat Minister for Home Affairs, who upon his appointment had reputedly declared that 'somebody has to be the butcher'. The design P.IX.1) shows an officer raising his glass above a street of butchered bodies with the caption 'Cheers Noske! the workers have been disarmed'. Grosz used his drawings from *Die Pleite* and *Der blutige Ernst* to satirize individuals such as Noske or Reichs Chancellor Ebert (Figure 16), and more general political themes such as capitalism or the military. These last two are the subject of the title page of *Die Pleite,* 1–6, 1920, in which two men hanging from gallows, a businessman and an army officer, wish each other 'A Happy New Year' (Pl.IX.27).

Other drawings could be seen to anticipate — or even encourage — revolutionary situations. One such illustration is his cover for *Der blutige Ernst*, 1–3, of 1919 (**Pl.IX.28**) which shows a workers' council sitting in judgement over a group of imprisoned army officers. Behind the 'judges' are views of factory chimneys, and a garlanded portrait of Karl Liebknecht. It represents a kind of revolutionary fantasy showing Grosz actively using his art as 'propaganda in the class struggle'. At this time Grosz believed that magazines and newspapers in particular had a positive role to play in the struggle against capitalism and the Social Democrats, for wide circulation and mass reproduction meant that his ideas could be widely disseminated. The success of Grosz's work for satirical weeklies led the Malik Verlag to publish a series of portfolios of his illustrations. Encouraged by Herzfelde, Grosz produced several controversial portfolios in the early 1920s based on social themes such as the plight of the working classes, the unacceptable faces of capitalism, profit, wars, brothels, and female prostitution.

The Malik Verlag portfolios

The Malik Verlag was a Marxist publishing house, although not the official press of the KPD. (To maintain its independence, Herzfelde actually refused financial support from the KPD and the Soviet Union – Irwin Lewis, p. 122.) Herzfelde's intention was to publish works that would encourage revolutionary attitudes and class consciousness among the working classes, hence a Malik series which appeared between 1920–3 called *The Little Revolutionary Library*. This consisted of eleven political and social studies and included a biography of Lenin and Grosz's portfolio, *The Face of the Ruling Class* (*Das Gesicht der Herrschenden Klasse*). Herzfelde also published works by Illya Ehrenberg, Tolstoy, Maxim Gorki, Trotsky and Georg Lukacs, and, later, Bertolt Brecht.

Because of its left-wing interests, Malik Verlag publications became a regular target of establishment critics. We saw that Herzfelde's first publication, the magazine *Neue Jugend*, which had appeared in 1916 had been banned by the censors. Grosz produced drawings for *Neue Jugend* that were published separately in a *First George Grosz Album* in 1917. After two issues which included contributions by Heartfield, the writer Franz Jung and the 'Dadaist' Huelsenbeck, this was also censored. To try to divert the attention of the censors, the publishing company assumed the name of Der Malik Verlag; Der Malik was the title of a harmless escapist story by the Expressionist poet, Else Laske-Schüler.

This cover had little effect and Herzfelde was continually taken to trial for his publications. The mere fact that Grosz's portfolios were published by Malik caused them to be viewed with suspicion by many parties within the government and the military, and on three occasions Grosz and Heartfield were tried for publishing drawings that were 'offensive' to the German people.

The way in which the portfolios were presented by Malik drew attention to the fact that they were often overtly political and seditious. Grosz did not usually draw sheets specifically for each book: most were selected from drawings already executed, and were grouped together around themes. Thus a collection of drawings grouped around, for example, the subject of the exploitation of the working classes and called *In the Shadows* (*Im Schatten*) was likely to have more impact than a single drawing on the theme which appeared in a magazine dealing with other issues.

In addition, some of those works which were re-used were given new titles or captions that made them more forceful in their characterization of the theme of the portfolio and generally gave them a stronger satirical edge. You can see how this works by taking away the caption from **Pl.IX.29** from the *God is on our Side* (*Gott* *mit Uns*) portfolio, published in June 1920. It shows an ugly and sadistic group of soldiers who outnumber and kill a group of insurgents, while two fat bourgeois sit eating in the foreground. With the caption *'The Communists are Dying and the Foreign Exchange Rates are Going Up'* the picture tells us more clearly that communists are being massacred to the satisfaction of two establishment figures, who are rejoicing at the (apparent) ensuing social stability which will send up the value of the mark. Military oppression against the workers is thus directly linked to the financial interests of capitalist society, a relationship which had been discussed in similar terms in Rosa Luxemburg's *Junius Bröschure* of 1916 and to which Grosz was probably making a reference. However, the portfolio was also published with foreign language titles, and these give slightly different emphases. The English title was *Blood is the Best Sauce* (after Goethe) and the French was *Ecrasez la Famine* (Fight Starvation). Thus the specific political reference was more clearly underlined to the German audience, although one could reasonably assume that most of the non-German purchasers of *God is on our Side* would understand all three languages, and that the foreign titles offered further opportunities to increase the number and type of ironic statements about the subject matter.

The *God is on our Side* portfolio, which contained nine lithographs (see **Pls.IX.29–32**), each with captions in German, French and English, satirized the relationship between the military and capitalism. The title *'Gott mit Uns'*, was a phrase stamped onto German soldiers' regulation belt buckles. Like *'The Communists are dying'* many drawings in this portfolio directly satirize the slaughter for which the army was responsible. In *Knocking-off Time* (**Pl.IX.30**) a soldier relaxes against a tree after a hard day's killing, and in the *Pimps of Death* (**Pl.IX.32**) grotesque members of the police and army stand in front of walking female skeletons, symbols of the slaughter and exploitation for which the former were responsible.

In the summer of 1920, shortly after publication, this portfolio was confiscated by police at the Dada fair, and the originals were confiscated from the Malik publishing headquarters on the instruction of the army. Grosz and Herzfelde were sent to trial for producing works that were insulting to the military. The proceedings of the trial were followed and criticized by the writer Kurt Tucholsky, whose comment:

> Either Grosz's drawings don't look like Reichswehr officers and therefore the Reichswehr was not insulted, or the officers look like Grosz's drawings and therefore Grosz is right,

did nothing to prevent the court from imposing a fine of 600 marks.

This portfolio, and the trial which it provoked, raises again the problem of defining and interpreting works that are ambiguously poised between using caricature and an illustrative or 'realist' style. While many contemporary critics and writers (particularly those associated with *Neue Sachlichkeit*) would have included these works within the broad label of 'realism' because of their figurative content, Grosz would probably have used the label to describe the additional propagandist function which, according to his many statements discussed earlier from this period, he intended such works to have. As we shall see, however, even Grosz's use of this label shifted according to his technical interests at the time.

The intended propagandist function of these drawings is achieved partly by the use of satire. Grosz has created stereotypes from those idiosyncrasies often associated with Prussian army officers, such as the moustache, the monocle, fatness and baldness. And the satirical impact of these drawings is greatly increased by the captions. Many of them had been published separately (some in *Der blutige Ernst* and *Die Pleite*) before being grouped together in this portfolio. But the meanings which they assumed (and the extent to which they were seen as 'propaganda') depended largely on the contexts in which they were consumed. To an army officer who believed that murdering insurgents was helping to restore stability to Germany and enforcing the power of the Social Democrats, this portfolio might have been (and was) seen as communist propaganda against the state; to a middle class liberal it might be seen as an educative and amusing satire on the army and its methods.

The following year Malik published a larger portfolio called *The Face of the Ruling Class* (**Pls.IX.29–36**), one of the earliest Malik portfolios specifically designed to educate and increase the class consciousness of the proletariat. It consisted of 55 lithographic reproductions in which Grosz depicted the greed, oppression, exploitation and hypocrisy which he had observed in the behaviour and interests of the post-war German bourgeoisie.

The nine *God is on our Side* lithographs were included in this portfolio. Reproductions included individual portrait stereotypes (**Pls. IX.33 and 34**) to which ironic or humorous titles such as '*There's a Smell of Riff-Raff around Here!*' were added. A large proportion of drawings in *The Face of the Ruling Class* represented an aspect of working class betrayal and exploitation by the German ruling class. In *At 5 o'clock in the Morning* (**Pl.IX.35**) Grosz uses the horizontal juxtaposition of two different scenes, the toiling workers and the fat carousing bourgeoisie, to suggest the profiteering and exploitative relationship of one to the other.

The Face of the Ruling Class was an outstanding success. The first edition of 6,000 copies was soon sold out and in the same year two more editions of 7,000 and 12,000 each were printed. It was avidly consumed by the very class it satirized: apart from the paperback edition at three marks (at the time of publication, three marks would buy about two eggs), low-priced to reach a working class audience, a hard-back edition sold for 15 marks, and a signed deluxe edition for the art collector was marketed at 100 marks. As the target here appeared to be a broad class of people rather than specific political figures or organizations, it was less susceptible to censorship. As long as they were not individually implicated, the middle classes could enjoy a satirical look at their own activities. However, Malik Verlag probably feared that this portfolio might lead to persecution, for in a review in the left-wing *Weltbühne* the editor Kurt Tucholsky urgently recommended that readers buy copies before the edition was confiscated by law.

Middle class greed and racketeering were also the subjects of the portfolio published in 1923 called *Ecce Homo,* which included 84 lithographs (**Pls.IX.3, 15, 26, 38, 41 and Figure 22**) and 16 watercolours (**Col.pls.IX.2,3,4,5 and Pls.IX.37, 39 and 40**). The works gathered together in this portfolio had been executed between 1915 and 1922, but their publication together in 1923, the year of galloping inflation in Germany, must have seemed particularly appropriate. Appendix C shows how many marks you could get for a dollar between June and November 1923. In June, one dollar was worth 100,000 marks but by the end of the year the dollar was worth over four billion marks!

Fortunes were made and lost overnight in Germany in 1923; corruption, illicit transactions and social chaos were rife. A Hungarian emigré, J. Dos Passos, who published with Malik and emigrated to the German capital after the war, has described his impression of Berlin at the time:

> The echoes of the Revolution were still there, with the rat-tat of a machine gun in the night and wildly hooting police cars. But the scene was dominated by the racketeer who seemed to wear a halo of gin-vapour and Havana cigar smoke. Money changed hands by the bushel and was available to finance almost any wildcat scheme. One could scarcely imagine that somewhere there were factories with workers toiling in them. On the one hand there was a mad pursuit of money and pleasure, carried on with the traditional German *Tüchtigkeit*; though joined by foreigners from all over Europe. In the cafés and night clubs, in an atmosphere of alcohol, tobacco smoke and cocaine, the racketeers were floating new companies with people they had never seen before.
>
> (J. Dos Passos, *George Grosz*, 1948, p. 11.)

Figure 22 George Grosz, Eva, 1918, from
Ecce Homo, 1923. © S.P.A.D.E.M.,
Paris, 1982.

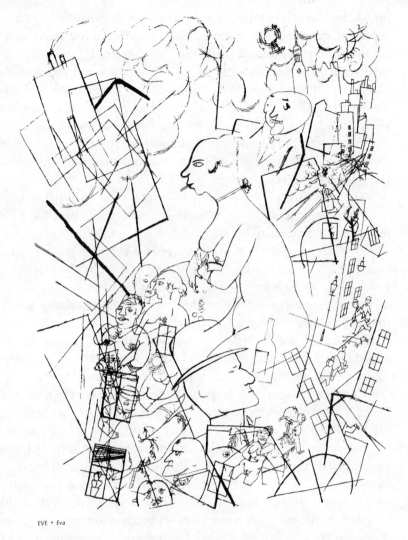

EVE · Eva

This vivid account underlines an important contemporary German preoccupation, to which much of Grosz's Berlin work was directly related. The capital city was increasingly seen as the symbol of the general moral corruption of Weimar Germany. It had the lowest birth rate of all European cities and was seen by conservatives as a den of moral laxity which symbolized the failure of the Republic. Cornelie Usborne has written:

> Berlin was witnessing, as Stefan Zweig put it, 'an orgiastic period, a feverishness of sexual activity and perversity' producing a moral panic not only in conservative, but also government, circles. Articles with headlines like 'pig killing in the brothel', 'nudist dances in the saddler's workshop' or 'a brothel in the train carriages', for example, were discussed in a session in the Ministry of the Interior. The government got so worried about excesses of public vice that Chancellor Cuno issued in February 1923 an emergency law to combat moral decay in public life.
>
> (From 'Population Control in Weimar Germany and the Question of Birth Control and Abortion', seminar given at the Institute of Historical Research, 12 March 1982.)

A large proportion of the *Ecce Homo* drawings and watercolours included references to female sexuality, brothels and prostitution, and Grosz himself became a victim of the 'moral panic' described above. He and Herzfelde were taken to trial again, this time for disseminating obscene pictures, and fined 6,000 marks.

▶ Look at **Col.pls.IX.2,4**, and 5 and **Pls.IX. 15, 37, 38, 39, 41 and 42** from the *Ecce Homo* portfolio.

1   How does Grosz represent women in these illustrations?

·2 Can a reading of these representations tell us anything about his and/or contemporary attitudes to prostitution? What sort of information would you need in order to draw parallels between such attitudes and Grosz's paintings and graphic works in this portfolio? ◄

▷ 1 You may have noticed that the drawings and watercolours in *Ecce Homo* were selected from works done between 1915–22, which may partly account for some of the differences in drawing style. It seems that there are several different types of images of women here. Some are more seductive and unsatirized than others. The heavy, voluptuous thighs of, for example, the watercolour, *Ecce Homo* (**Col.pl.IX.2**) which gave the portfolio its title, are more erotic than caricatured. Many, however, are represented as grotesque, predatory figures, as in *Beauty, I Thee Praise* (**Pl.IX.42**). And others are clearly degraded, exploited or violently abused physically, as in *Dr. Benn's Night Spot* or *Sex Murder* (**Pls.IX.15 and 41**).

It is difficult to find one clear moral theme which underlies these different representations, although some of the subjects can be related to specific interests in Grosz's life. The detective stories of the old 'penny dreadfuls', which Grosz had avidly consumed in his youth, were full of dramatic sex murders, themes that dominated some of his early drawings from around 1912. And Hans Hess wrote (*George Grosz*, p.38) that 'crime, murder, suicide and rape had a strange attraction for Grosz that was to last most of his life'. During different periods of his work, however, Grosz seems to have been attracted to these subjects for different reasons. He had followed the sex murders of the 'penny dreadfuls' because of their interest as escapist dramas, while his later interest in brothel life as represented in *Ecce Homo* could be seen (as argued later) to be directly related to contemporary social and political developments in Weimar Germany.

Whether they are being seductive or the victims of rape, women in the *Ecce Homo* portfolio are usually presented in some state of undress; the clothed woman whose nakedness is revealed underneath (**Col.pls.IX. 3, 4 and Pls.IX. 37 and 39**) seems to be Grosz's usual means for signifying prostitution. And many of his images distort the female anatomy, creating grotesque and dehumanized bodies as in *Lying In* (**Pl.IX.39**). There were well-established conventions in German 'Expressionist' painting for the representation of distorted or seemingly deformed female forms: the Brücke group had become well-known for angular, deformed nude studies of women which, as in the work of Kirchner, often included the representation of prostitutes and 'women of vice' (see Television Programme 10 and Block IV). In Grosz's work, which was probably influenced by this tradition, prostitutes were frequently represented as grotesquely distorted and dehumanized, suggesting that he saw the theme as a metaphor of a corrupt society and its broader social problems.

2 Before being equipped to answer the second part of this exercise, we need to know something about both Grosz's own and contemporary German attitudes to prostitution. In the immediate post-war years it was an issue extensively covered by the popular press, becoming a focus of political activity and debate. In her research on this aspect of post-war Berlin life, C. Usborne has claimed that while post-war ministerial reports estimated that there were roughly 6,000 registered prostitutes under police surveillance, there were at least ten times this number roaming the streets who were not on the books of the 'moral' police. (The population of Berlin at the time was around 2 million.) The social upheavals of the war and constant troop movements had been accompanied by a dramatic increase in the vice trade. The increase was monitored through the escalating numbers of people suffering from venereal diseases, the spread of which was generally attributed to prostitution. And in the early twenties galloping inflation made German centres, of which Berlin became notorious, immensely attractive to foreigners whose foreign currency could buy them night life and 'vice' on the cheap.

The German 'revolution' of 1918 had been accompanied by a marked relaxation of moral codes, a growth in more libertarian attitudes towards sex outside marriage, female sexuality and prostitution. In the early twenties, then, the exploitation and conditions of prostitutes became the concern of many social reformers and feminist groups, who sought to change the prostitution laws:

> Section 361/6 of the German Criminal Code stated that prostitution was not a punishable offence if the prostitute was registered with the police and subjected to regular health checks and treatment for venereal disease. In practice, this meant that the 'moral police' patrolling the inner city streets could arrest any woman whom they suspected of being a prostitute, force her to have a medical examination and if this proved that she was suffering from VD have her officially registered as a 'woman trading in vice'. This system was devised to ensure that the dreaded 'social disease' was kept to a minimum, since prostitution could not be banned. As it supplied a need that was regarded to be too powerful to be banned by even the most draconian penalties, the least the state could do was to guarantee that the 'goods' were in a healthy condition. This state regulation of prostitution had been opposed passionately by the abolitionist branch of the German Women's Movement since the 1890s. What enraged feminists and male reformers alike were the facts that (a) it was the women, not the men, who were held responsible for extramarital intercourse and suffered the consequences, and (b) that it was a case of women of the poorer strata being exploited by middle and upper class men.
>
> (C. Usborne; taken from notes for her Ph.D thesis.)

An important and controversial bill to combat VD was put forward in 1919, which included a clause relating to prostitution. This bill sought to free prostitutes from police regulation, transferring the responsibility for health checks to municipal welfare authorities, with women doctors in charge. When it was eventually passed after many stormy debates by the lower house of the Reichstag in 1922, it was vetoed by the upper house (the Reichsrat) because the prostitution clause proved to be too libertarian to be passed by right-wing politicians. Even though all parties were agreed in principle on the urgency of the VD bill, arguments on the regulation of prostitution delayed the final passing until 1 October 1927 when:

> State-regulated prostitution was finally abolished, the 'moral' police disbanded, the system of restricting prostitutes' dwellings to certain streets or houses made illegal. Instead of police threats and penalties the new emphasis was on social hygiene, moral education and social re-integration.
>
> (C. Usborne *op.cit.*)

Thus during the first half of the 1920s the problem of prostitution, so much evident on Berlin streets, was constantly debated in political and journalistic circles. While conservatives, who were against the bill, tended to see the problem as part of a 'sexual bolshevism' which had taken over society during the early days of the Weimar Republic, the communists saw the problem as one of capitalist exploitation of working class women, and therefore supported the bill.

As Grosz did not write about his specific intentions regarding individual works in *Ecce Homo*, we have to be careful about oversimplifying the links between this material and a contemporary political issue such as prostitution. However, we can assume that the tremendous publicity which the issue generated, and the problems involved in trying to get a reforming bill through the German parliament probably encouraged Grosz and Herzfelde to publish the *Ecce Homo* portfolio in which the more satirical drawings could be seen to contribute to the debate. In view of the controversy in the Reichstag in 1923, they could not have chosen a better year. It could also be argued that there are more specific aspects of this contemporary debate as outlined above that could be seen to be represented in the images shown in some of Grosz's work from this portfolio.

It seems that the issue of class exploitation is one that recurs in many of Grosz's

Ecce Homo illustrations on the theme of prostitution. His stereotyped representations of the bourgeoisie such as the fat cigar-smoking capitalist or the balding monocled Prussian businessman, are usually the consumers, as in the debauched proceedings of *Waltz Dream* (**Col.pl.IX.4**), *Ecce Homo* (**Col.pl.IX.2**) or the negotiations taking place in *Before Sunrise* (**Pl.IX.37**). In these illustrations Grosz seems to echo the attacks of many contemporary social reformers on the hypocrisy of prevailing bourgeois values, Such values expected middle class girls to maintain their virginity before marriage while young bachelors and married men were encouraged to seek sexual satisfaction and experience by exploiting the availability and financial needs of working class prostitutes.

The exploitation that takes place through the activities of pimps or middlemen is also satirized in illustrations such as the watercolour, *White Slaver* (**Col.pl.IX.5**), in which the central figure is an affluent bowler-hatted figure, profiteering at the expense of his 'white slaves' in the background. In *Lying In* (**Pl.IX.39**) it is also possible that Grosz is making a reference to the problem which dominated so much contemporary debate: the spread of venereal diseases. Beneath a grotesque half-naked woman is a hideously deformed new-born baby, perhaps included as a recognizable symbol of the effects of syphilis, a theme that had already preoccupied writers and artists popular in pre-war Germany, including Heinrich Ibsen and Edvard Munch (see Radiovision Programme 10).

Grosz's interest in the subject of prostitution is rooted, then, in the specific social and political context of Berlin during the Weimar period. And the theme was one that preoccupied many other German painters and illustrators from this period who were concerned with contemporary social issues, and with whom he associated.

Grosz and *Neue Sachlichkeit* in the mid-1920s

From the mid-1920s onwards the work of Otto Dix and George Grosz (among others) was frequently included by critics within the loose group label, *Neue Sachlichkeit*. This is usually translated into English as New Objectivity or New Realism, although the German meaning is more specific. As John Willett has written: 'Its quality of '*Sachlichkeit*' implies objectivity in the sense of a neutral, sober, matter-of-fact approach, thus coming to embrace functionalism, utility, absence of decorative frills' (*The New Sobriety*, p. 112). The term, which also came to be used to describe developments in literature, was first coined by G.F. Hartlaub, the director of Mannheim Kunsthalle, where he organized an exhibition under the title '*Neue Sachlichkeit — Deutsche Malerei seit dem Expressionismus*' ('German Painting since Expressionism') in the summer of 1925. The show had originally been intended to cover European movements but eventually restricted itself to German. Thirty-two artists exhibited, including George Grosz, Otto Dix, Max Beckmann, Alexander Kanoldt, Georg Scholz, Georg Schrimpf and Karl Hubbuch (**Pls.IX.24 and 43**). In May 1923 Hartlaub had sent out a circular to artists, art critics and dealers asking for contributors to his forthcoming exhibition:

> In the autumn I would like to mount a medium-sized exhibition of paintings and graphic art which might perhaps have the title '*Die Neue Sachlichkeit*'. I am interested in bringing together representative works by those artists who over the last ten years have been neither Impressionistically vague nor Expressionistically abstract, neither sensuously superficial nor constructivistically introverted. I want to show those artists who have remained — or who have once more become — avowedly faithful to positive, tangible reality.
> (Arts Council, *Neue Sachlichkeit and German Realism of the Twenties*, p.9.)

Hartlaub's preoccupation was, then, with some kind of new 'realism' which broke with the more introverted and abstract characteristics of Expressionism. But his use of the label was in some respects similar to Roger Fry's use of the term Post-Impressionism for the first Post-Impressionist Exhibition held in London in 1910 (see Radiovision Programme 24). Although used to denote very different stylistic groupings, both were categories devised by the exhibition organizers and which imposed a framework of art historical meaning on the exhibitors. *Neue Sachlichkeit*, as we shall see, gave the exhibiting artists a status as a coherent group with similar aims. As a new label it also gave them the status of a new movement, as the sequel to (an equally diffuse) 'Expressionism'.

Hartlaub's 1923 circular went on to qualify his label, distinguishing between 'right' and 'left' wings in the movement:

> It is necessary to consider the right-wing (Neo-Classicists, if you like), as in certain things by Picasso, Nebel, etc., and also the left, Veristic wing, which includes people like Beckmann, Grosz, Dix, Scholz, etc. . . .

Although Hartlaub was using 'right' and 'left' primarily as art historical labels, he chose them because of their political connotations, especially in relation to the German 'Veristic wing'. But the political implications of Hartlaub's 'left' and 'right' categories do not always have clear relevance to the pictures they are being used to describe. While aspects of Grosz's work (particularly his graphics) from the early twenties are conscious pieces of left-wing political propaganda, the work of Max Beckmann (see Television Programme 21) from this period fits less easily into such a category. And Picasso's position within the 'right' wing is to do with an apparently neo-classical 'realism' which Hartlaub also identified in the work of the Italian painters Giorgio de Chirico and Carlo Carrà, whose '*Pittura Metafisica*' or 'Metaphysical Painting', which influenced many contemporary German painters, used strange figurative imagery with classical associations.

In 1925 Franz Roh, one of Hartlaub's advisers on the Mannheim *Neue Sachlichkeit* Exhibition, published a book that developed a similar view of contemporary European and German art: *Post-Expressionism: Magic Realism, Problems of the Most Recent European Painting*. An edited chapter from this is reproduced as *Supplementary Documents*, IX.6, and is discussed in Part 3, where we will consider in more detail the theoretical problems involved in such attempts to establish a coherent modern theory of 'realism'. Roh's category of 'Magic Realism' had similar frames of reference to Hartlaub's *Neue Sachlichkeit*. Roh's category denoted a new European art heavily indebted to Italian Metaphysical Painting, which, he believed, had rejected 'Expressionism' in favour of a return to more realistic representation, to what he called a renewed 'contact with the object world'. Roh argues that this tendency is especially pronounced in Germany, where he also uses the label 'Verism' for the work of Dix, Grosz, Scholz, Karl Hubbuch and Rudolf Schlichter (**Col.pl.IX.8** and **Pls.IX. 21–24, 43 and 44**), i.e. those artists whom he considered were more concerned with contemporary social issues in their work.

There were three paintings by Grosz in the Mannheim Exhibition. These included the *Little Sex Murderer*, 1918, (also known as *John, the Sex Murderer*) (**Col.pl.IX.6**) and the *Portrait of Max Hermann-Neisse*, 1925 (**Col.pl.IX.7**).

▶ 1   Look at these plates: are there any characteristics which relate (if at all) to Hartlaub's definition of *Neue Sachlichkeit* quoted at the beginning of this section?

2   Do these two works share characteristics of style and subject matter with the following works by Otto Dix and Georg Scholz, whom Hartlaub grouped with Grosz as representing the 'left wing' of the *Neue Sachlichkeit* movement: Dix, *Three Prostitutes* (**Pl.IX.21**), Dix, *Portrait of Flechtheim* (**Col.pl.IX.8**), and Scholz, *Industrialized Peasants* (**Pl.IX.24**)? ◀

▷ 1   There are marked differences in style in the two Grosz paintings, which represent different periods in his work. The construction of *The Sex Murderer*, painted seven years earlier than the portrait, is similar to that of Grosz's Dada collages which are peopled by stylized geometrical figures (see Radiovision Programme 19). The strong diagonal rhythms and overlapping planes also recur in other works from this period and reflect the influence of Italian Futurist conventions discussed earlier.

The *Portrait of Max Hermann-Neisse* was one of Grosz's first oil paintings from the mid-1920s (he had largely abandoned this medium in the preceding years). It is a more detailed, illusionistic representation of this subject than *The Sex Murderer* and seems therefore to be more easily encompassed within Hartlaub's notion of the depiction of a 'tangible reality'. Hermann-Neisse was a writer who had supported Grosz during the *Ecce Homo* trial, and who became a close personal friend. In 1925–6 Grosz worked on many similar portrait sketches and paintings of family, friends (Col.pl.IX.7) and figures he admired, such as the German boxing champion Max Schmeling (Col.pl.IX.10).

In these later portraits Grosz appears to have been more concerned with a technique of painting in which actual brushwork is disguised and is therefore more likely to suggest a naturalistic illusion. The *Portrait of Max Hermann-Neisse* appears more highly finished and more detailed than *The Sex Murderer,* in which loose areas of brushwork are clearly visible. In the earlier work Grosz was more concerned to make a statement on a contemporary social problem, whereas his many portrait studies from the mid-1920s, which represent friends rather than political figures, and are more conventional easel paintings, are clearly less appropriate vehicles for making social or political statements. Thus Hartlaub's notion of a left wing within the *Neue Sachlichkeit* movement is further confused, for the works by Grosz which seem to be more appropriately described by Hartlaub's more 'realistic' form of painting are also those works that were less consciously political.

2   A detailed and seemingly highly finished quality of painting, similar to the *Portrait of Max Hermann-Neisse* also characterizes Otto Dix's *Portrait of Alfred Flechtheim*, 1926 (Col.pl.IX.8). In both portraits the artists take their detailed 'realism' to the point of exaggeration of recognizable features. The facial features are closely observed but almost irreverently represented, a quality of exaggeration that echoes the techniques of political cartoons, while Georg Scholz uses a similarly detailed technique in his oil and collage *Industrialized Peasants* (Pl.IX.24), but the images which this technique describes are clearly not 'realistic' in any photographic sense; the grotesque faces of the peasants are broken by images of screws and money. These, like other juxtapositions of images in the painting are used to make a point about the bigotry and greed of German farmers who profited in the post-war years from urban food shortages. Grosz uses a similar pictorial device in the symbolically sawn-off or open head in his *Pillars of Society*, 1926 (Col.pl.IX.9).

Grosz, Dix and Scholz were three of the artists grouped by Roh in the German 'Verist' wing of a new 'realist' movement. There are, as we have seen, some clear associations between the styles and themes employed by these artists, but the 'Verism' grouping also more clearly reflects their shared political interests. Grosz, Scholz, Rudolf Schlichter and John Heartfield had formed with others a Red Group (*Rote Gruppe*) or Union of Communist Artists of Germany in 1924, with which Dix became associated when he moved to Berlin in 1925. The group manifesto outlined their intention to work closely with the KPD to increase and strengthen communist propaganda. ◁

Both the themes and techniques of painting which Grosz adopted in the mid-1920s have, however, been seen to represent a shift in his political interests. The polemical tone of earlier satirical paintings such as *Burial; Dedicated to Oscar Panizza*

(Col.pl.IX.1) is absent in most of his portraits of friends and colleagues from 1925–6. This shift in emphasis has also been identified in his drawings. Until 1924 Grosz had published almost exclusively with Malik Verlag but in 1925 he began to publish less overtly political drawings with other more moderate publishers. In 1925, for example, he published a collection of sixty drawings, *Mirror of the Philistine* (*Spiesser Spiegel*) (Figure 23) with the Reissner Verlag. Although the themes are similar, these lacked the frequently ironic captions of the Malik portfolios, the drawing style is generally less satirical (i.e. physical types are less exaggerated) and the use of line less clear and precise.

Figure 23 Page 8 from the portfolio, Spiesser Spiegel (Mirror of the Philistine), *1925. From B. Irwin Lewis,* George Grosz: Art and Politics in the Weimar Republic, *University of Wisconsin Press, 1971, p.178.* ©*S.P.A.D.E.M., Paris, 1982.*

Many accounts of Grosz's work have seen in these changes a direct reflection of the contemporary political situation. By 1923 he had returned somewhat disillusioned from Russia, and in October of that year the communists had unsuccessfully tried to seize power, been outlawed, and subsequently devoted their energies to reorganizing the party. Irwin Lewis has written:

> Grosz reflected the communists' loss of revolutionary ardor in his drawings. Grosz's commitment to communism was tied to the terror and tumult of the first year of the republic. With the visible foe, the Free Corps, underground, political assassinations waning, unemployment slowly decreasing as the economy was stabilized, and the government changing through elections and parliamentary reshuffling instead of revolts and putsches, Grosz's aggressive zeal was tempered and his artistic talents were diverted into different channels.
>
> (Irwin Lewis, *op.cit.*, p.175.)

However, there are no clear-cut causal links between developments in the KPD and changes in Grosz's drawing and painting style. Evidence suggests that there are many complex — though not necessarily unrelated — possible reasons for these changes.

In 1925, the year that his work was shown in the Mannheim Exhibition, Grosz was helping to launch the Red Group (mentioned earlier) and published with Herzfelde a group of articles in a book *Art is in Danger*. This included many articles already published but an important essay in the book was based on Grosz's article 'Evolving' (*'Abwicklung'*) written in 1924. This set out Grosz's and Herzfelde's interpretation of a Marxist view of history and the role of the artist within that history. Within western capitalist society they identified only two real alternatives for the modern artist:

> Art is in danger. Today's artist, unless he wants to be useless, an antiquated misfit, can only choose between technology and class war propaganda. In either case he must give up 'pure art'.
>
> (*Art is in Danger*' op.cit.)

Thus at a time when Grosz's painted and graphic work could be seen to have lost some of its overtly political edge, he was writing as vehemently as ever for a revolutionary propagandist art, for an effective *Tendenzkunst*.

Given this ambivalence, there are other possible reasons for the changes in Grosz's style at the time. After the financial and popular success of the Malik portfolios, Grosz was well established as an artist and illustrator and his work was likely to arouse the interest of the larger German publishing houses, who were able to pay higher royalties. Success had also attracted the patronage and interest of the wealthy Berlin gallery owner Alfred Flechtheim, who became his dealer and gave him a one-man show in 1923. Flechtheim rarely showed German works; his was one of the most important Berlin galleries exhibiting French Modernist works. (In Otto Dix's portrait of Flechtheim (**Col.pl.IX.8**) you will notice that the dealer is shown holding two paintings which look like synthetic Cubist works.) To be shown by Flechtheim was a mark of artistic and social distinction. It also encouraged Grosz's work to be seen within a modern European context as representative of a modern German movement.

It could also be argued, of course, that the stabilizing political situation in Germany in the mid-1920s was a factor that helped to provide a social environment in which dealers and publishers such as Flechtheim were more likely to commission work and pay higher fees. Flechtheim's patronage and friendship at that time may have helped to persuade Grosz to return to more conventional forms of easel painting. For an established artist, portrait painting could provide a lucrative source of commissions and income. Thus Grosz was commissioned by Flechtheim to paint the portrait of Max Schmeling (**Col.pl.IX.10**), and his portrait of Hermann-Neisse was purchased for 2,500 marks by the Mannheim Kunsthalle during the *Neue Sachlichkeit* exhibition.

Flechtheim also owned and edited a monthly literary magazine called *Der Querschnitt* (*Cross-Section*) in which Grosz was regularly represented through drawings and watercolours. The magazine was a more liberal publication than those of Malik Verlag, which may be a reason why Flechtheim selected and commissioned those works which, like *The Best Years of Their Lives* (**Pl.IX.45**) lacked the more cutting political irony of many of the Malik illustrations.

Grosz's painted and graphic work from the so-called *Neue Sachlichkeit* period (i.e. the mid-1920s) reveal complex interests which are not all directly explained by his political activities and reactions to political developments at the time. When seen in relation to his writings, this work suggests an ambivalent attitude towards finding a formal language that could convey a political meaning. And the problem clearly was not resolved in the notion of a 'left wing' within the *Neue Sachlichkeit* movement. As we have seen, those paintings which were exhibited by Grosz and grouped under that label were in some ways less overtly 'political' than the satirical drawings which he published in his early Malik portfolios.

Grosz and theatre set designs in the late 1920s

In the mid–late 1920s Grosz's political interests played an important role in his attitudes towards and production of theatre set designs. Between 1919–28 he designed sets and/or costumes for several Berlin theatre productions. He collaborated with John Heartfield on the sets for several shows, including Shaw's *Caesar and Cleopatra* in 1920, Georg Kaiser's *Clerk Krehler* in 1922 and Shaw's *Androcles and the Lion* in 1924. In 1924 Grosz began to work with the director Erwin Piscator, a personal friend since they had both belonged to the Berlin Dada group. In the 1920s Piscator was concerned to develop an effective left-wing theatre, experimenting in his performances with technical devices such as slides, film, and sets influenced by Constructivist conventions, which would increase the didactic and political effect of his plays.

Piscator identified his work with the traditions and ideals of the German *Volksbühne* (People's Theatre), which produced good plays at affordable prices and was designed to serve the local community. Unlike the English theatre at the beginning of this century, Germany had a long tradition of left-wing theatre groups, whose activities were suppressed during the period of anti-socialist laws of 1887–90. After World War I, the Weimar Republic provided a relatively tolerant political atmosphere in which such a tradition could re-emerge (albeit interrupted by frequent law suits). In this environment the idea of the theatre as a place of political education rather than simple entertainment could re-establish itself.

Bertolt Brecht began his career as a dramatist after the First World War, at a time when communist dramatists, such as Ernst Toller, were writing plays that related to contemporary political issues (for example, Toller's *Masses and Man*, 1919, traces the problems of a revolutionary whose humanism places her in a dilemma regarding the use of violence).

Many of the debates which predominated in this area of German drama were similar to those which preoccupied Grosz and other left-wing artists during the post-war period. These included the Marxist debates on how the classless society was to come about, or be brought about, and how the theatre was to be used in this cause. Through his work with Piscator, Grosz saw the theatre as an area in which drama and graphic art could and *should* be inextricably linked to promote political education. In 1926 he worked with Piscator on a production of Paul Zech's *Das trunkene Schiff* (literally translated as *The Drunken Boat,* from Rimbaud's *Le Bâteau Ivre*) at the *Volksbühne*, for which they projected drawings onto three screens surrounding the actors. In the following year Piscator commissioned Grosz to design drawings, to be projected in a similar way, for the backcloth to his production of *The Good Soldier Schweik* which opened in January 1928. The play was adapted largely by Brecht from the novel *Schweik* by the Czech writer Jaroslav Hašek. Schweik, who is called up for war service, becomes the näive victim of military sadism, corruption and authoritarianism. Grosz made several hundred drawings from Hašek's story. These were used for cut-out figures and an animated film for projection onto the backcloth (**Pls.IX.46–51**). In 1928 Malik published seventeen of these drawings in a portfolio called *Hintergrund (Background)*. In that year Grosz wrote enthusiastically of Piscator's theatre and its potential for a politically committed graphic artist:

> It is a fact that here Erwin had created a great new area for the graphic artist to work in, a veritable graphic arena, more tempting for graphic artists of today than all that stuffy aesthetic business or the hawking around of drawings in bibliophile editions for educated nobs. Here's a chance for our often quoted latter-day Daumiers to paint gloomy prophecies on the walls.
>
> What a medium, though, for the artist who wants to speak to the masses, purely and simply. Naturally a new area requires new techniques, a new clear and concise

language of graphic style — certainly a great opportunity for teaching discipline to the muddle-headed and confused! And there's nothing to be achieved with your careless impressionist rush, either. The line must be cinematographic — clear, simple, but not too thick, because of over-exposure; furthermore it must be hard, something like the drawings and woodcuts in Gothic block books, or the massive stone carvings on the pyramids.

(*Blätter der Piscatorbühne* (*Journal of the Piscator Stage*), 1928 ; trans. in U. Schneede, *op. cit.*, p. 108.)

▶ Look at Grosz's designs for this production (**Pls.IX.46–51**). What strikes you about these drawings? Do they fit Grosz's descriptions quoted above of the function of design in Piscator's drama? ◀

▷ Grosz wrote excitedly about the new type of theatre that Piscator had created, a medium that demands a clear didactic graphic style. Thus most of Grosz's cartoons use simple linear designs which could be projected onto the backcloth screens. For this performance Piscator used moving floors on which the actors were conveyed through various theatrical situations. He also used a screen as a backdrop onto which film of Grosz's cartoons was projected, providing a visual commentary on the action. These projected images also allowed Piscator to extend the historical relevance of the production using images such as 'Be submissive to the Authorities' which satirized the Austrian and German military (joining hands in the foreground), the Law (represented by a skeletal judge) and the Clergy (who balanced a cross on his nose).

Although most of the set designs use simple black outlines you will probably have noticed differences in the styles of some of the designs. Many are brush and ink, although some, such as *Lt. Lukatsch's Living Room* (**Pl.IX.51**) incorporate actual photographs. Unlike Heartfield's photomontages, in which shapes and images are intercut (see Radiovision Programme 20 and associated plates), this is organized to look like a personal collection of photographs. Postcards arranged in a semi-circle over two crossed swords show women in various stages of undress, a clear reference to the lieutenant's fantasies. This combination of drawn and photographic images linked with Berlin Dada activities, was used throughout the performance; Piscator frequently projected Grosz's drawings with film footage of contemporary events. Other variations in Grosz's technique relate to the technical devices used in the stage production. The thickly drawn 'S' shape of *The Tree of Life* (**Pl.IX.49**) was transformed into an image of a man strangled by a giant paragraph sign. The images were projected in sequence to create the effect of a continual metamorphosis. Despite the changing pictures, all have the same underlying theme which appears as a subtitle to *The Tree of Life:* 'Freedom is a bourgeois preconception'.

Grosz argued that his technique had to be concise and clear not only for its didactic function within the theatre, but also because it must 'speak to the masses'. By this he meant that the images must be easily readable and accessible to an ordinary working class audience. However, on this point it is worth noting that the presentation of selected designs from the *Schweik* production in the Malik portfolio *Hintergrund* could have a significant effect on the received meanings of these works. Those images which a theatre audience would have seen as backcloths or illustrations to the play were given extended or often ironic titles that broadened their meaning. For example, the *Schweik* design, *Inspection* (**Pl.IX.48**), was published in *Hintergrund* with the caption 'The entire population is a bunch of malingerers'.

On one level, however, Grosz's claim was borne out by the success of Piscator's performance. According to contemporary reports it was well-attended, and the success of this performance was cited ten years later by Brecht in his essay 'Popularity and Realism' (Reader, Text 35) which challenged the views held by the left-wing critic Georg Lukacs on the nature of Socialist Realism. This essay is discussed in more detail in Part 3, but briefly Brecht rejected Lukacs' advocacy of a nineteenth-century 'realist' tradition, in favour of new modes of 'realistic' representation which should utilize some of the innovations of modernism. He argued that these new conventions could be rendered both accessible and popular in the context of the theatre, as was proven (he believed) by the success of his own and Piscator's theatrical experiments, in which 'conventional forms were constantly destroyed'. He also argued that this form of drama had found its greatest support in the 'most advanced cadres of the working class':

> The workers judged everything according to the truth of its content; they welcomed every innovation which helped the representation of truth, of the real mechanism of society; they rejected everything that seemed theatrical, technical equipment that merely worked for its own sake – that is to say, that did not yet fulfil, or no longer fulfilled, its purpose.

> (B. Brecht, *Popularity and Realism* – see Reader, Text 35.)

As this was written in retrospect, Brecht may have exaggerated the working class response to the *Schweik* production, assuming perhaps that all KPD supporters were necessarily working class. While the play attracted wide public interest and support, it was *after* a selection of the drawings had been published in *Hintergrund* that Grosz and Herzfelde were accused of blasphemy and the drawings confiscated. The trial was directed specifically at three drawings which included '*Shut Up and Soldier On*' (**Pl.IX.46**) and '*Be Submissive to the Authorities*' (**Pl.IX.47**). The trial which lasted from 1928–31 was moved from court to court and involved a series of sentences and appeals. It was closely followed by intellectuals and the press and at the end of the trial the drawing '*Shut Up and Soldier On*' was destroyed. Grosz, however, got off with only a fine. According to records of the trial, one of the central issues was a disagreement over the interpretation of the title. These works were either being spoken by Christ – which constituted blasphemy – or were being addressed to him. Grosz argued that if Christ had 'come down again to preach the gospel in wartime he would have been faced with the cruel command "*Shut Up and Soldier On*"'. (Records of court proceedings, 10 December 1928.)

Once again Grosz's work was directly affected by censorship laws instituted by a government anxious to combat a much-publicized 'moral decay' in contemporary German society, a 'decay' which had already been identified in several of Grosz's Malik portfolios.

3 Art history and criticism on Grosz and Weimar art

In the preceding sections we have already touched on the issue that dominated so much of the contemporary debates among left-wing artists in Weimar Germany: what was the function of an artist working in the socialist movement within German capitalist society, and what form should his/her art practices take? A part of this section will consider these debates, looking closely at Grosz's own statements on the subject, at some of the disputes with other artists' groups with which he became involved, and at subsequent attempts in Germany in the 1920s–1930s to develop coherent theories of socialist art and its relationship to contemporary 'culture'.

The theme of Grosz and Weimar has tended to attract critical approaches that are not clearly identifiable as Modernist (in the sense in which writings by Fry or Bell are). As his Weimar work has often been seen as offering a positive alternative to Modernism, it has attracted (particularly in recent years) a body of criticism which is itself self-consciously anti-Modernist. The issues raised by his work (i.e. the specific subjects selected and the manner in which they are represented) demand a different critical framework to that of Modernism, if they are to be treated as other than marginal to the central line of development.

There was, however, a body of writing produced in Europe and America in the 1930s–1940s which, despite attempts to anchor Grosz's work in an 'anti-fascist' culture, was rooted in a Modernist critical tradition.

▶ Read the following extracts from accounts of Grosz's *Ecce Homo* portfolio discussed earlier. Both are by American critics. The first is from a 1934 essay on Grosz by Thomas Craven; the second is taken from a monograph of 1971 on Grosz and Weimar by Beth Irwin Lewis.

1   {*Ecce Homo*} – the most effectual cutting instrument in modern art. You may never see this book, and more's the pity; for it stands among social chronicles as a work of unapproachable realism . . . .
Ecce Homo may be termed the Anatomy of Degradation. It is neither erotic nor obscene; it is profoundly and surgically explicit. In line, the more incisive because of its economy; in watercolour of acid strength, the book presents a culture gone hog-wild; a society once composed and cleanly, abandoned to its most ignoble instincts. We might say that the only cure for such a society is to let it die of its own excesses; but Grosz thought differently about it; he was aware that the wallowing vitality of the Germans was not decadence but stupration – and capable of satire, he was not without hope . . . .
One might think in viewing this picture, that the German ideal, if it may be so denominated, was universal and unproductive copulation. And when I say that Grosz is explicit, I mean that he does not scruple to set down everything necessary to a complete record; not only the human body in any attitude or situation, but all its parts, minutely studied and drawn, and organically functioning. Behold the man!
The record is truthful, as those historically informed will certify. Knowing the period, you will say, 'That is Germany!' Knowing art you will say 'That is Grosz!'

Imaginatively conceived and bearing on every page the stamp of an individual point of view, *Ecce Homo* passes from biological satire into the realm of art. For art is interesting in proportion to the richness of the personality behind it, and the personality is formed from direct and integrated experiences.

(Thomas Craven, 'George Grosz' in *Modern Art: The Men, the Movements, the Meaning,* Simon & Schuster, N.Y., 1934, pp.204 *ff.*)

2   Many people have looked at the *Ecce Homo* and have found in it a brilliant document of the night life in Berlin during the inflationary period of the early twenties. Further, it has been said that the *Ecce Homo* was the product of an artist of Prussian Protestant upbringing who was repulsed by the libertarian nature of the society in Berlin. According to one of his friends, Grosz represented the pure Protestant believer who could not accept sin or evil with any of the grace or romanticism of the Roman Catholic. No longer theological or even theistic, the Protestant mission against sin turned into political polemic and propaganda in Grosz's work. But fundamentally it was still the voice of the eternal Protestant raging against this earthly world.

There is much truth in these views, but they miss an essential point about *Ecce Homo*. It was drawn by George Grosz, a Marxist whose avowed purpose was to use art as a weapon against the classes that oppressed the proletariat. *Ecce Homo* was a '*document humaine*' in the tradition of Goya, Degas, and Toulouse-Lautrec, but it was also eroticism in the service of communist propaganda.

While *Ecce Homo* was not polemical in the sense that *Abrechnung folgt*** was, it had a definite political purpose. It was an attack on the bourgeoisie. By depicting the bourgeois as a degraded class wallowing in copulation and coition, Grosz could expose their moral hypocrisy. In these drawings Grosz presented a Marxist vision of dehumanization which takes place within the capitalist society: man has become an object and he treats others as objects.

*'The Reckoning Follows', 1923. This was another Malik portfolio which concentrated on themes similar to those in *The Face of the Ruling Class*.

(Beth Irwin Lewis, *George Grosz: Art and Politics in the Weimar Republic,* University of Wisconsin Press, 1971, pp. 163–66.)

In what ways do these two approaches differ? Which do you find the most useful for an understanding of Grosz's work and interests at the time? ◀

▷ Craven sees *Ecce Homo* as an honest reflection – an exposure – of Berlin night life, as 'a work of unapproachable realism'. Craven's notion of 'realism' is tied to the belief that Grosz is giving us a full and truthful record of things as they were. At the same time Craven is anxious to consolidate a Modernist view of Grosz as a highly gifted individual. The 'realm of art' which, he implies, is part of individual expression, passes beyond satire; it is to do with the richness of the personality who produces it. Craven's account provides little information on the context in which the portfolio was produced, the contemporary social and political issues to which the illustrations are addressed or the ways in which they might have been read at the time. It is a personal – and at times almost poetic – description of the images as the critic sees them, with a concluding paragraph which firmly places the emphasis on Grosz as a unique individual.

It is significant that this account was written at a time when Grosz was living in America and had rejected many of his earlier political ideals and more 'propagandist' works. His later autobiographical writings had tended to play down the political commitment involved in the production of earlier drawings, and Craven even writes of the earlier political commitment, in a section of this chapter (not reproduced above), that 'Grosz himself today is even a little appalled by it' (p. 212).

Irwin Lewis, writing in America in the 1970s, takes a different position. While acknowledging that the portfolio forms a document of Berlin night life in the early 1920s and a possible expression of attitudes formed through Grosz's Protestant background, she is also concerned to relate *Ecce Homo* to Grosz's interests and preoccupations at the time. Published when Grosz was a committed member of the KPD, it is seen by Irwin Lewis as a work which was produced as propaganda, and which reveals in its imagery a Marxist analysis of society. Her approach is closer to that taken in this block, in that we have argued that the themes and modes of presentation of those themes must be seen in relation to Grosz's interests and preoccupations at the time, the aims and activities of Malik Verlag, and contemporary social issues and debates. It could be argued, however, that she oversimplifies some of the details involved in the production of *Ecce Home* in order to make her point more forcefully. We saw earlier that the drawings and watercolours which made up this portfolio were selected from works done between 1915–22, and in some cases it was the addition or rewriting of a caption that made the illustration more clearly satirical or propagandist. ◁

The view that Grosz's portfolios from the early 1920s were propagandist in that they presented a Marxist view of the class divisions in contemporary society was shared by Grosz himself in his writings from this period. One of his earliest written statements of his views on art was provoked by an incident in Dresden in the spring of 1920. On 15 March a battle between the workers and the *Reichswehr* had taken place in the central Ostplatz. Fifty-nine people died and many were injured, and, in the firing, bullets had entered the Swinger Gallery damaging Rubens' *Bathseba*. The president of the Dresden Academy, the painter Oscar Kokoschka, issued a series of posters and manifestoes pleading with the Dresden public to engage in such confrontation in places where the safety of 'sacred heirlooms' might not be threatened. One of these published statements, addressed 'To all Inhabitants of Dresden' is reproduced as Appendix E, with a retrospective comment by Kokoschka on his statement and those events.

Please read Appendix E. You will note that Kokoschka's declarations under-lined the idea that Germany's collection of masterpieces was a sacred heritage which should have a status above politics, and which was vital for the cultural future of German society.

In response to these attitudes, Grosz and John Heartfield published an emotion-al article entitled 'The Artist as Scab' ('*Der Kunstlump*') in *Der Gegner*, No. 1, 1919. They questioned Kokoschka's fundamental assumption that art works were 'sacred heirlooms' of the German people, arguing that such 'heirlooms' and their preserva-tion represented one aspect of the control of the proletariat by the bourgeoisie. The nation's value should be measured by its productive people, not by its art works. The damaged Rubens was of little significance in relation to the proletarian deaths which the Dresden conflict had caused. The article had a strong polemical tone and several of its main arguments were developed in Grosz's essay, *Instead of a Biography*, published in August of that year.

▶ Read this short essay reproduced in *Supplementary Documents, IX.3*. Briefly summarize the main points in the essay. Are any problems raised by these ideas on 'proletarian art' ◀

▷ This essay reinforces the point made in 'The Artist as Scab' that art and culture are in the service of the bourgeoisie; they become over-valued as part of a capitalist market in which they are exchanged for profit. The artist is dependent on collectors and dealers for whom value lies in the cult of the individual 'genius'.

Modern artists have, according to Grosz, perpetuated this cult claiming to be the exponents of spiritual and metaphysical values, and by so doing have isolated themselves from the real world. The revolutionary status attributed to so many modern artists is therefore seen as a hoax. They are merely consolidating a bourgeois ideology. Grosz appealed to artists to use their work as weapons in the class struggle, to actively support the proletariat through their art. As a Marxist, Grosz believed that there could not be an eternal and isolated category called 'art', for this itself is a bourgeois construction.

This essay raises significant theoretical and practical problems for artists to whom Grosz was appealing. According to crude Marxist theory (sometimes called reflectionist theory) the art or 'culture' produced by a society is ultimately controlled and produced by the class which owns the means of production, and must inevitably reflect this class ideology. It follows from this view, which was held by many members of the KPD, that no real proletarian culture could evolve within a system in which the economic power base was controlled by capitalism. You saw in the preceding block that similar arguments were raised when forms and conventions were sought that could adequately represent revolutionary and post-revolutionary situations. ◁

In his written statements, Grosz does not, however, confront this problem in any coherent theoretical form. It was through the writings of Brecht and Walter Benjamin later in the 1920s and 1930s that clearer theoretical positions were evolved, with which Grosz became indirectly associated. These challenged a vulgar Marxist view of 'culture' as an unmediated and inevitable reflection of bourgeois political interests. We will return to these writings later in this section.

What kind of activity then did Grosz himself advocate for the radical artist working within a Weimar framework?

In his essay, *My New Pictures* (*Supplementary Documents*, IX.5) written in 1920 and published in *Das Kunstblatt*, 1921, Grosz describes the style that he was using at the time to convey his revolutionary ideas. He argued that individualistic styles, often justified by metaphysical claims, were inaccessible to ordinary people and that he was trying instead to give a realistic picture of the world:

> I am trying in my so-called works of art to construct something with a completely realistic foundation. Man is no longer an individual to be examined in some subtle psychological terms, but a collective, almost mechanical concept. Individual destiny no longer matters.

This professed attempt to depersonalize his work is a direct reference to the style of the five illustrations from 1920 which accompanied *My New Pictures* in the *Kunstblatt* article (e.g. **Pl.IX.2**). They all employ a precise naturalistic style directly influenced by the Italian school of '*Pittura Metafisica*' (Grosz specifically mentions a member of this school, Carlo Carrà). The figures are faceless mechanical constructions, and line is used according to Grosz 'in an impersonal way to construct volumes'. Grosz believed that this style provided an alternative to Expressionist fantasies, that it possessed an objectivity similar to that of an 'engineer's drawings'.

You have probably noticed some contradictions in this and the preceding article. Grosz's mechanical style, as described in *My New Pictures* and illustrated in the pictures that originally accompanied it, is rather different to the biting satirical drawings of, for example, the Malik portfolios, in which individual political figures are often the target of attack. The depersonalized 'automatons' of the *Kunstblatt* series were likely to have less impact in a class war than caricatures of recognizable politicians and social groups.

Grosz himself seems to have recognized these contradictions for he soon abandoned his supposedly objective style, publishing only a few similar works. Grosz adopted the style when he was associated with the Berlin Dada movement. Like many German intellectuals and fellow members of the Dada group (see Radiovision Programme 19) and the KPD, Grosz had been closely following developments in modern Russian art, and was influenced by some aspects of the Russian Constructivist movement in his use of clearly structured compositions and rectangular shapes.

It should also be noted here that a Modernist art historian might argue that one of the reasons why Grosz failed to produce an effective 'revolutionary' style was because he was not really a painter. He was primarily a graphic artist who, unlike some contemporary Russian 'Constructivists', could not fully exploit the 'revolutionary' potential of the formal means of painting.

But what Grosz's experiments and their subsequent rejection show is that the issue of a formal language which could convey the intended relationship between art and politics was problematic, and that there were no specific technical or iconographical properties which could guarantee for art a specific political meaning. Many of the debates on this problem were implicated in the issue of a contemporary 'realism', particularly the forms of 'realism' associated with the label *Neue Sachlichkeit*.

Neue Sachlichkeit and art criticism

Modernist histories of twentieth-century art have generally given little attention to the so-called *Neue Sachlichkeit* movement, placing more importance on German Expressionist movements of the post-war period, particularly the work of Kandinsky, Klee and the Bauhaus. For example, Herbert Read's *History of Modern Painting*, published in 1959, includes only one short paragraph on *Neue Sachlichkeit* in a book which otherwise has extensive coverage of German movements. But the extent of German writing on the subject in the twenties suggests that it was then seen as a more important development in the history of German art than subsequent Modernist accounts would lead us to believe. The figurative and 'realist' styles associated with *Neue Sachlichkeit* don't fit easily into a linear Modernist account of the development of an 'autonomous' abstract art. For this reason, many surveys of modern art which have included sections on *Neue Sachlichkeit* have tended to separate it clearly from contemporary avant-garde developments in Germany. Thus Hamilton discusses 'Art in Germany 1920–40' in a separate chapter that covers Italy, Holland, Belgium and Austria, and which is entitled 'Independent Schools and Masters' (p. 473, *ff*).

We saw in Part 2 how the label *Neue Sachlichkeit,* first coined by Hartlaub for the 1925 Mannheim Exhibition, was a broad label of convenience. We also saw how the critic Franz Roh devised an alternative category, 'Magic Realism', of which a sub-category of German realist art was labelled 'Verism'.

▶ Read the chapter on German 'Verism' from Roh's book *Post-Expressionism* (*Supplementary Documents,* IX.6). How does Roh understand and use the category 'Verism'? What stylistic and/or political interests does he identify within this grouping? ◀

▷ You might have felt that in his argument on the nature of Verism Roh often tries to encompass contradictory characteristics. He argues that German Verism 'offers faithfully an unfragmented portrayal of nature' or 'iron-hard objectivity'. But he is also concerned with a curious notion of the self-expression of the object world, with the idea that visual facts can somehow express themselves (a notion reminiscent of some Expressionist theories of 'expressive forms' – see Block IV). He also claims that the specific themes represented by German artists in their attacks on contemporary social life (e.g. the underworld, the brothel) are more general symbols. These artists, he believes, would paint such themes irrespective of the social and political situations in which they found themselves. Roh, then, is suggesting these artists possess a persistent will to paint certain themes, irrespective of their historical context.

Roh is determined to identify historical precedents for what he calls the 'Activist' wing (which includes Grosz and Dix) of Verism, identifying Hogarth, Daumier and Toulouse-Lautrec as evidence of an historical lineage and 'timeless attitude'. In the Grosz and Daumier comparison in the Introduction to this block, we emphasized that despite similar uses of satirical conventions, the two works (i.e. *White General/Conqueror*) could only be effectively understood in their respective historical contexts. Similar arguments could be used to counter Roh's assumption that German 'Activism' is merely the continuation of a supposedly timeless set of art historical interests.

He clearly feels ambivalent about the work of the 'Activists', questioning the notion of *Tendenzkunst* discussed earlier. To legitimize his attempts to embrace both a left and right wing within his grouping 'Verism', he seeks to undermine the possible political interpretations of Grosz's work. Roh argues that the political meanings of Grosz's work constitute only a superficial layer of meaning, and he identifies three more significant layers:

1   the quality of the graphic work;

2   the supposedly 'unpleasant' depiction of the proletariat; and

3   the contradictory aspects of Grosz's writings on man's nature.

In view of points 2 and 3, he argues that political readings of Grosz's work are not always helpful. In time, he believes the subject matter will lose its significance while the qualities of graphic technique will assume greater importance, an argument which is close to that of many Modernist theorists already considered in this course.

In critical usage in the 1920s Roh's category of Magic Realism was usually interchangeable with Hartlaub's *Neue Sachlichkeit*, although more recent criticism has tended to use *Neue Sachlichkeit* to denote what Roh called the left or Verist wing of the movement. However, the Marxist critic Helmut Lethen (who was a member of the Frankfurt school which we discuss below) has used the term *Neue Sachlichkeit* to represent what he saw as the *right* wing of the movement. In a collection of essays, *New Objectivity 1924–32 – Studies in the Literature of White Socialism*, published in 1970, Helmut Lethen understands *Sachlichkeit* as a form of bourgeois liberal thought characteristic of the period of economic and political stabilization in the late 1920s. According to *his* argument the 'committed' or left wing of the movement, including artists like Grosz and Dix, came under the 'Verist' label. ◁

The debates about what forms of *Neue Sachlichkeit* or new 'realism' constituted a radical political art were taken up by many German Marxists in the 1920s–1930s. An intellectual Marxist tradition was well established in Germany in the early 1920s with the founding of the Frankfurt Institute for Social Research in 1923*, a privately funded (and therefore relatively independent of government) institution with links with the German labour movement. Interestingly, one of the private financiers was Felix Weil, a friend of Grosz who had also helped finance the Malik Verlag and Piscator's theatre. Members of the Frankfurt school evolved theories of culture and cultural production that challenged those of the official left, which was thought to be degenerating into 'economism' (or crude economic determinism). They formulated Marxist theories, many of which, in very broad terms, were more rooted in the traditions of German philosophical idealism and which were influ-

*With Hitler's accession to the German Chancellorship in 1933, it moved to America.

enced in the early 1920s by the writings of Georg Lukacs. The main theorists of the Frankfurt school, who included Theodor Adorno and Herbert Marcuse were concerned with a broad historical notion of cultural production and what they called the modern 'culture industry'. Although many of their arguments were developed in relation to literature (as with Marcuse) or music (as with Adorno) some of the fundamental issues raised are relevant to our discussion of the visual arts.

The writings of Georg Lukacs were an influential intellectual force in German Marxist circles during the early years of the Frankfurt school. In his *History and Class Consciousness*, published in 1923, he formulated a Marxist position heavily influenced by a Hegelian view of history; according to Lukacs' argument, single moments of history are understood as the means whereby the historical process is drawn towards its foreseeable end. He claimed, for example, that the Russian proletarian revolution had provided the 'moment' of history or the 'missing link' through which bourgeois philosophy with its humanist ideals might be realized, or put into practice.

In later writings, especially those from the 1930s (see E. Bloch *et al., Aesthetics and Politics*, London, New Left Books, 1978) Lukacs developed a theory of 'Critical Realism' which was based on this view of history. Like many Frankfurt theorists he looked to the nineteenth century for those forms of bourgeois culture which should be sustained in the twentieth century, which should be 'realized' in modern history through 'moments' in the historical process. You saw in Block VIII, Part 3, that Lukacs came to advocate an art based on a bourgeois tradition of 'critical realism', exemplified, he believed, in the work of Balzac. It would be useful if you re-read the relevant pages of Block VIII at this point. You should have noted that Balzac's own ideological position, his own politics, were not thought to undermine a Marxist reading of his works. Balzac's characters were seen as 'typical' of their class, hence Lukacs' notion of 'typicality' which was opposed to a vulgar Marxist notion of mere 'symbols' of class. Lukacs, who was working in Russia in the 1930s (he worked in the Moscow Marx-Engels Institute in 1930–1 and in the Philosophical Institute of the Moscow Academy of Sciences from 1933–4), was thus arguing for a form of 'Socialist Realism', albeit based on a more sophisticated notion of 'realism' than that which was held by many Russian party members in the 1930s, and which Briony Fer discussed in Block VIII.

Lukacs' views were challenged in the 1930s from another position in the writings of Brecht, who was a personal friend of Grosz. Brecht's arguments, which are set out in his essay, 'Popularity and Realism' (Reader, Text 35) revolve around the relative meanings which he gives to 'formalism' and 'realism'. We saw in discussion of Piscator's *Good Soldier Schweik* that Brecht argued in this essay that new formal conventions were necessary in drama (as in literature) to represent a constantly changing social reality. He believed that 'realism' is not a static concept, and need not therefore be derived from existing works; it should represent the complexities of contemporary social reality. According to this argument, Balzac's form of novel writing cannot be used to provide a model (i.e. an a-historical model) for subsequent epochs. Thus he writes:

> Realism means: discovering the causal complexities of society/unmasking the prevailing view of things as the view of those who are in power/writing from the standpoint of the class which offers the broadest solutions for the pressing difficulties in which human society is caught up/emphasizing the element of development/making possible the concrete, and making possible abstraction from it.
>
> ('Popularity and Realism'.)

Brecht's concept of 'realism', then, allows him to utilize some conventions which, as he himself points out, have been associated with Expressionism. He does not share the wholehearted rejection of Expressionism of many of his Marxist colleagues (which included many members of the Frankfurt school). Brecht believed that some forms of fruitful 'experimentation' have emerged from Expressionism and could be absorbed into a 'realist' approach:

> For me expressionism is not merely an 'embarrassing business', not merely a deviation. Why? Because I do not by any means consider it to be merely a 'phenomenon' and stick a label on it. Realists who are willing to learn and look for the practical side of things could learn a great deal from it.
>
> (B. Brecht, *On the Formalistic Character of the Theory of Realism,* reproduced in E. Bloch, *op.cit.*)

Brecht argued that Lukacs' adherence to the old forms of nineteenth-century 'realist' literature was itself a 'formalist' preoccupation, that past modes of representation could constitute an *un*realistic formalism, because they did not conform to a changing contemporary reality.

An important concern which underlies Brecht's essay 'Popularity and Realism' (Reader, Text 35) is the relationship of production to consumption in the artistic process. Like his friend and colleague Walter Benjamin, Brecht emphasized the *cognitive* function of art as the central factor for consideration in its production. He argued that the way in which the work of art is produced is determined by the interests of the working masses who consume it. Because of this fundamental assumption Brecht believed that 'realism' and what he called 'popular art' must be closely allied:

> Popular means: intelligible to the broad masses, adopting and enriching their forms of expression/assuming their standpoint, confirming and correcting it/representing the most progressive section of the people so that it can assume leadership, and therefore intelligible to other sections of the people as well/relating to traditions and developing them.

Walter Benjamin, in his essays 'The Author as Producer', 1937 (Reader, Text 32) and 'The Work of Art in the Age of Mechanical Reproduction', 1936 (Reader, Text 33) developed Brecht's arguments in relation to visual works of art. Both essays were discussed briefly in Block VIII, Part 3. You will recall that in 'Author as Producer' Benjamin rejects a crude Marxist argument that a work of art produced within a capitalist society must inevitably reflect capitalist social relations. He shifts the emphasis from asking: what is the attitude of the work to the relations of production of its time? to asking what is the position of the work within these relations? By shifting the emphasis Benjamin can concern himself with a notion of relative autonomy, in that the artist is in a position to mediate these relations, rather than produce a crude reflection of them. The artist's role, according to Benjamin, must be that of a producer working within a collective social framework, rather than an isolated 'creative genius'. In this framework his/her alignment with the working class must not merely be one of social attitude, but must also involve a technical change or difference. If solidarity with the proletariat does not go beyond political attitude, the work of art could have a counter-revolutionary function, as was demonstrated, he believed, by what he calls 'Activism' and *Neue Sachlichkeit* in literature (you will note that Benjamin's use of the term 'Activism' is therefore rather different to Franz Roh's). In the visual arts, on the other hand, he argued that the photomontages of John Heartfield, some aspects of Dada and Surrealism were examples of work which had an effective revolutionary function, produced with a view to their public consumption, and in which technical progress is seen (echoing Brecht) as 'the foundation of political progress'. (In Radiovision Programme 19, Dawn Ades briefly discusses Benjamin's attitude towards Dada.)

Conclusion

In considering Grosz's work and activities during the Weimar period we have seen that there was no one contemporary form of pictorial 'realism' which was universally recognized as a 'Marxist art', or even more loosely as a 'political art'. We have seen that even within German Marxist circles and traditions in the 1920s and 1930s there were differing theoretical positions on the forms which a 'Marxist art' should, or could, take.

The theoretical writings of Brecht and Benjamin which we have discussed were written in the 1930s after the Weimar period, and cannot therefore be considered in direct relationship to Grosz's work from that earlier period. However, his friendship in the mid-1920s with Brecht, Piscator and intellectual circles associated with the contemporary German theatre, encouraged his interest in the technical possibilities for combining a 'political art' with 'political theatre'. Through these interests and his connections with the KPD and Malik Verlag, he was familiar with the contemporary debates which surrounded attempts to find a 'political' art form, although (as we have seen) his own writings from the 1920s lack the theoretical coherence of those of some of his contemporaries. It is, perhaps, ironic that it was not until Grosz had emigrated to America, where he changed both his graphic style and his views on art, that Brecht and Benjamin formulated and published theories which provided the critical tools through which Grosz could justify and explain his borrowings from Modernist conventions, while also maintaining that his work had a political or propagandist function.

In seeking to understand what the contemporary meanings of Grosz's works might have been in the 1920s, we have tried to look closely at the political and historical circumstances in which they were produced, at the peculiar 'historical conjuncture' of Weimar Germany at the time. We have attempted to show how the impetus for the various forms of so-called 'revolutionary art' discussed in this block was at least partly created by the specific social, political and economic upheavals, the revolutionary and counter-revolutionary developments and ensuing growth in forms of political awareness, in post-war Weimar Germany.

References and further reading

Works marked with an asterisk are recommended further reading and should be available in a good library.

Arts Council, *Neue Sachlichkeit and German Realism of the Twenties*, Hayward Gallery, London, 1979.

Bloch, E., *et al.*, *Aesthetics and Politics*, New Left Books, London, 1978.

Bittner, H., *George Grosz*, Arts Inc., New York, 1960.

Busch-Reisinger Museum, *Theatrical Drawings and Watercolours by George Grosz*, Harvard University, 1973.

Craig, G.A., *Germany 1866–1945*, Oxford University Press, 1981.

Craven, T., 'George Grosz' in *Modern Art: the Men, the Movements, the Meaning*, Simon Schuster, New York, 1934.

Dorner, A., 'Grosz, Post-War Pilgrim's Progress', in *Art News*, Vol. 40, 1941, No. 5.

Dos Passos, J. and Hofbauer, I., *George Grosz*, Nicholson and Watson, London and Brussels, 1948.

Eksteins, M., *The Limits of Reason – The German Democratic Press and the Collapse of Weimar Democracy*, Oxford University Press, 1975.

*Gay, P., *Weimar Culture*, Penguin, London, 1968.

Grosz, George, Poem in *Almanach der Neuen Jugend auf das Jahr 1917*, Malik Verlag, Berlin, p. 144.

Grosz, George, 'Der Kunstlump' (The Artist as Scab') (with John Heartfield) in *Der Gegner*, Vol. 1, Nos. 10–12, pp. 48–56, Malik Verlag, Berlin *c.* 1919. Reprinted in *Die Aktion*, Vol. 10, columns 327–32, Verlag der Wochenschrift Die Aktion, Berlin, 1920.

Grosz, George, 'Statt einer Biographie' ('Instead of a Biography'), Berlin, 16 August 1920, in *Der Gegner*, Vol. 2, No. 3, pp. 68–70, Malik Verlag, Berlin 1920–21 (see Reader, Text 3).

Grosz, George, 'Abwicklung' ('Evolving'), *Das Kunstblatt*, Vol. 8, No. 2, February, 8 illustrations, Verlag Gustav Kiepenheuer, Berlin 1924, pp. 32–38.

Grosz, George, *Die Kunst ist in Gefahr* ('Art is in Danger') (with Wieland Herzfelde) *Drei Aufsätze* (3 essays) 'Die Kunst ist in Gefahr! Ein Orientierungsversuch', pp. 33–38, 'Paris als Kunststadt', pp. 33–38, 'Statt einer Biographie', pp. 39–45, vol. e Malik–Bücherei, Malik Verlag, Berlin 1925, and Russian Edition, State Publishing House, Moscow, 1926.

Grosz, George, *A Little Yes and a Big No: The Autobiography of George Grosz*. Translated by Lola Sachs Dorin, 38 plates and numerous text drawings, The Dial Press, New York 1946.

Hamann, R. and Hermand, J., *Expressionismus*, Akademie-Verlag, Berlin, 1977.

Hoffmann, E., *Kokoschka: Life and Work*, Faber, 1943.

Hess, H., *George Grosz*, Studio Vista, 1974.

*Irwin Lewis, B., *George Grosz – Art and Politics in the Weimar Republic*, University of Wisconsin Press, 1971.

Count Kessler, *Diaries of a Cosmopolitan*, Weidenfeld and Nicholson, London, 1971.

Kunstamt Kreuzberg, Berlin, and the Institut für Theatrewissenschaft der Universität Köln, *Weimarer Republik*, Elefanten Press, GmbH, 1977.

Miesel V.H. (ed.), *Voices of German Expressionism*, Prentice-Hall, New Jersey, 1970.

Needle, J. and Thompson, P., *Brecht*, Basil Blackwell, Oxford, 1981.

Ryder, A.J., *The German Revolution 1918–19*, The Historical Association, 1971.

Schneede, U.M., *George Grosz – His Life and Work*, translated by Susanne Flatauer, Gordon Fraser, London, 1979.

Usborne, C., 'Population Policy in Weimar Germany and the Question of Birth Control and Abortion', paper given at the Institute of Historical Research, 12 March 1982.

Usborne, C., Notes for Ph.D thesis 'The Politics of Fertility Control in Germany 1912–27'.

Willett, J., *Expressionism*, World University Library, Wiedenfeld and Nicholson, London, 1970.

*Willett, J., *The New Sobriety: Art and Politics in the Weimar Period 1917–33*, Thames and Hudson, London, 1979.

Appendix A

Outline of events — Grosz and Germany up to 1933

(*Note:* this provides only a brief outline of developments in German history, along with a chronological summary of Grosz's activities. Fuller details on German history during the twentieth century can be found in James Joll, *Europe since 1870, and International History*, (recommended reading for the course) — chapters 5, 8, 9.)

1909	September: Grosz at the Royal Academy, Dresden.
1912	Moved to Berlin where he attended the *Kunstgewerbeschule.*
1913	August-November: Grosz's first visit to Paris.
1914	3 August: Germany declared war on France. On 4 August: the Reichstag approved the mobilization and the political parties agreed initially to a truce. Extensive war loans began to threaten the stability of German currency structure. 11 November: Grosz volunteered for the German army.
1915	11 May: Grosz discharged as unfit for military service.
1916	29 August: Wilhelm II appointed Hindenburg and Ludendorff to head of the supreme command of the army. 31 August: Hindenburg programme is drawn up which called for the doubling of munitions production and trebling of production of cannon and machine guns by spring 1917.
1916–17	Winter: allied naval blockade caused serious deterioration of the food situation, heavy rationing and widespread starvation.
1917	4 January: Grosz was called up again, but admitted to a military hospital on 5 January. Permanently discharged from the army in May and returned to Berlin. There was growing opposition in Germany to the war loans; and increasing disagreements within the SPD (German Social Democrats.) April: a parliamentary group breaks away from SPD to establish itself as an independent party called the USPD (Independent Social Democratic Party of Germany). This included Rosa Luxemburg, Clara Zetkin and Karl Liebknecht. First Grosz portfolio (*Erste G. Grosz Mappe*) of 20 lithographs published in Berlin.
1918	Grosz took part in the first Berlin Dada activities. By September, Germany's allies, the Turks and Bulgarians, were falling to the Allied forces; the Austrian Empire was collapsing and German efforts in France were thwarted by Allied reinforcements from America. The German High Command was demoralized and General Ludendorff demanded that the Berlin government should secure an armistice to preserve the army. October: despite serious losses the German naval command planned another attack against the English forces, causing a mutiny in the navy. The events which followed became known as the *November Revolution.* 3 November: at Kiel, workers and soldiers declared their solidarity with sailors and set up a list of social and political demands including termination of the war and universal suffrage. A series of workers' councils were then formed in most large German towns. 9 November: Wilhelm II abdicated. The office of Reichs Chancellor was transferred to Friedrich Ebert, president of the SPD and the German Republic was established. Also on 9 November Karl Liebknecht proclaimed the Socialist Republic, and listed a series of demands including shorter working hours, a fixed minimum wage, reform of the army and expropriation of funds owned by mines, steel industries and banks. 10 November: a government of the 'Council of Representatives of the People' was formed from members of the SPD and USPD. On the same day General Groener (Ludendorff's successor) made a pact with Ebert. The imperial army was to be absorbed into the *Reichswehr* and was to help in the suppression of left-wing socialists, but in return it was to play a part in the political administration of the country.

11 November: the 'Spartacus League', led by Liebknecht and Luxemburg, was founded, although it remained a group within the USPD.

31 December: Spartacists split from USPD to form the German Communist Party (KPD). Grosz, Wieland Herzfelde, John Heartfield and Erwin Piscator were among founder members.

1919   5 January: German Workers' Party (DAP) founded. From March 1920 this was to become the National Socialist German Workers' Party. In September 1919 the DAP was joined by Lance-Corporal Adolf Hitler.

5 January: a revolt against the government, supported by the Communist Party, was initiated by the occupation by workers of the publishing houses of Ulstein, Mosse and Scherl, the SPD newspaper *Vorwärts*, railway stations and the Reich printing works.

6 January: General strike called. Over the next 10 days the uprising was violently put down, mostly by the notorious *Freikorps*, led by Noske. Both Liebknecht and Luxemburg were arrested and murdered.

19 January: elections took place for a German National Assembly. Women were given the vote for the first time. SPD polled the highest number of votes (11.5 million).

February: Friedrich Ebert elected Reichs Chancellor by the National Assembly. In the same month there was increasing concern among workers over the government's lack of progress in implementing a promised programme of socialist policies. By mid-February a strike movement had started in the Ruhr. Strikes were put down by *Freikorps* and Security Police, but a general strike was called on 1 March, causing a series of bloody confrontations. Social Democrats were increasingly attacked from the political right because of their agreement to the terms of the Treaty of Versailles, which demanded large reductions in the German army and navy.

March: the Kapp Putsch, an attempted coup of the radical right occupied government buildings and tried to establish Wolfgang Kapp as Reichs Chancellor. The coup failed through lack of support. The unions declared another general strike and the government agreed to reshuffle members, dismissing Noske, and to nationalize several major industries.

1920   Grosz put on trial (with Herzfelde) for publication of his Malik portfolio *God is on our Side* and fined 600 marks.

1921   Grosz published his Malik portfolio *The Face of the Ruling Class*.

1922   Grosz spent 5 months in USSR where he met Lenin.

1923   Inflation, which had been accelerating since the end of the war, reached its peak when the exchange rate for one US dollar = 4.2 billion paper marks (see Appendix C). Grosz published *Ecce Homo* with Malik Verlag, and is taken to trial for publishing obscene drawings.
Autumn: KPD is outlawed.
November: Hitler organized an unsuccessful putsch against the government. The National Socialist German Workers' Party was temporarily disbanded.

1924   1 April: Hitler sentenced to 5 years' imprisonment, but granted an amnesty towards the end of the year. Grosz became chairman of the *Rote Gruppe* (Red Group), an association of communist artists. Second *Ecce Homo* trial took place and Grosz was fined 500 marks for publishing obscene pictures.

1925   Hindenburg, candidate of the coalition of parties of the right, was elected Reichs Chancellor

1928   Grosz accused of blasphemy in his portfolio of drawings *Hintergrund*.

1931   Under the leadership of Hitler, Hugenberg, Seldte, and General von der Goltz, National Socialists, and other right-wing organizations were combined to form the 'Harzburg Front'. In October the Front demanded the resignation of the government, and pronounced itself ready to seize power.

1932   Spring: the Harzburg Front collapsed as a result of an internal struggle over Hitler's imminent election as Reichs Chancellor.

1933   30 January: Hitler appointed Reichs Chancellor and head of the coalition government.

Appendix B

Financial cost of war to the German Reich, 1914–18

(From F.W. Henning, *Das Industrialisierte Deutschland 1914–1972*, Paderborn 1974, p. 42.)

Year	War Expenses in Billion Marks	War Loans in Billion Marks	Totals for each year in Billion Marks
1914	7	0.2	7.2
1915	23	1.1	24.1
1916	27	2.3	29.3
1917	40	4.2	44.2
1918	50	9.2	59.2
Totals	147	17	164

Appendix C

Value of the German mark against the US dollar in 1923

June 1923	$1	=	100,000 marks
July 1923	$1	=	350,000 marks
August 1923	$1	=	4,600,000 marks
September 1923	$1	=	100,000,000 marks
October 1923	$1	=	25,000,000,000 marks
November 1923	$1	=	4,200,000,000,000 marks

Appendix D

Distribution of seats in Reichstag elections of 1920

Party	No. of Parliamentary Seats
Social Demokratische Partei (SPD).	113
Zentrums Partei (Zentrum).	67
Deutsche Demokratische Partei (DDP).	45
Deutsche Nationale Volkspartei (DNVP) (former conservatives; the most right-wing nationalistic party).	66
Deutsche Volkspartei (DVP) (former national liberals; became overtly right-wing after *c.* 1929).	62
Kommunistische Partei (KPD).	2
Unabhang Social Demokratische Partei (USPD).	81
Bayer Bauerns Bund.	4
Hannover USW Landsparteien.	5
Bayer Volkspartei (with Christliche Volkspartei) (centrist coalition).	21

From: *Statistische der Deutschen Reiches*, Bd. 291/1, Heft 1, pp. 4–5.

Appendix E

Statements by Kokoschka

Published statement issued by Oscar Kokoschka, then president of the Dresden Academy, in the spring of 1920:

> I direct the following request to all who propose in future to resort to firearms to argue for their political theories, whether of the left or the right or the radical centre: that they cease to stage these military exercises in the tilt-yard in front of the art galley, and hold them on firing ranges in open country, where human culture is not put at risk. I do not dare to hope that my alternative proposal will prevail: that in the German Republic, as in classical times, feuds might henceforth be settled by single combat between political leaders, perhaps in the Sarassani Circus, made more impressive by Homeric catcalls from the parties which they 'command'.

Kokoschka later made the following comment on this statement:

> This manifesto I issued in the spring of 1920 after the German Communist Revolution had been defeated in Berlin, in the industrial districts and in Saxony, Bavaria and Hamburg. I saw the street-fighting of the workers, glamourized in the intellectual circles while the victims of the blunders of the Comintern policies were doomed to failure not only for theoretical reasons that the Social Democrats considered the Communists to be the only real danger to them. Democracy had to bind its eyes while the counter-revolution of the united world monopolies made Europe step by step safe against collective socialist doctrine and international creed which threatened to get the mass support of the proletarized society of the West as well as in the East. Quite naturally German Social Democracy had to ask for foreign loans in order to rebuild its industry. No country with no capital invested abroad can live without exporting industrial products in exchange for foodstuffs and raw materials. Only Great Britain, as the international broker, lived on the interests from British capital invested abroad. Thus, in 1920, the combination of circumstances and events conditioned the birth of National Socialism in Germany, where the principle of rationalization of the monopolies was adopted for the first time in its most dramatic form, challenging humanism. Whether rationalization will allow recognition of the fact that the conservation of the human race is necessarily a condition if only for the sake of preserving the economic prosperity of war industry and its future, will be left for consideration to these monopolies standing behind all capitalist governments.

(From E. Hoffmann, *Kokoschka: Life and Work,* Faber, 1943, p. 143.)